pursuing
holiness

A small group resource developed from
In Search of Holiness and Practical Holiness

pursuing holiness

A small group resource developed from
In Search of Holiness and *Practical Holiness*

By David K. Bernard

WORD AFLAME PRESS
HAZELWOOD, MO

Pursuing Holiness
by David K. Bernard

© Copyright 2013 David K. Bernard

Published by Word Aflame Press, 8855 Dunn Road, Hazelwood, MO 63042. Printed in the United States of America.

All Scripture quotations in this book are from the King James Version of the Bible unless otherwise identified.

Scripture quotations marked NKJV taken from the New King James Version®, Copyright © 1982 by Thomas Nelson, Inc. Used by permission. All rights reserved.
Scripture quotations marked NIV are taken from the HOLY BIBLE, NEW INTERNATIONAL VERSION®. NIV®. Copyright © 1973, 1978, 1984 by International Bible Society. Used by permission of Zondervan Publishing House. All rights reserved.

All rights reserved. No portion of this publication may be reproduced, stored in an electronic system or transmitted in any form or by any means, electronic, mechanical, photocopy, recording, or otherwise, without the prior permission of Word Aflame Press. Brief quotations may be used in literary reviews.

Library of Congress Cataloging-in-Publication Data

Bernard, David K., 1956-
  Pursuing holiness / David K. Bernard.
    pages cm
  ISBN 978-1-56722-976-9
1. Holiness--Pentecostal churches. 2. Oneness Pentecostal churches--Doctrines. 3. Pentecostal churches--Doctrines. 4. Christian life--Pentecostal authors. I. Title.
  BT767.B473 2013
  248.4'8994--dc23
                    2012051597

Contents

Session 1

1 A Call to Holiness 11

Discussion Questions 27

Session 2

2 The Dangers of Legalism 31

3 Christian Liberty 47

Discussion Questions 61

Session 3

4 The Christian Life 65

5 Christian Attitudes 77

Discussion Questions 92

Session 4

6 The Tongue: An Unruly Member 95

7 The Eye: The Light of the Body 113

Discussion Questions 124

Session 5

8 Scriptural Apparel and Adornment 127

9 Bible Truths Concerning Hair 143

Discussion Questions 155

Session 6

10 The Temple of God 159

11 Sexual Relationships 173

Discussion Questions 193

Preface

Since the release of David K. Bernard's *In Search of Holiness* and *Practical Holiness*, over 150,000 of his works on holiness have been distributed. The sincere, balanced voice of this trusted author and leader continues to provide direction to Christians in our search to understand how to live a life pleasing to God.

This new volume is a compilation of *In Search of Holiness* and *Practical Holiness*, following the author's direction. It presents a revised study of selected material from each volume. Discussion questions are included at the end of each chapter for use in a group setting or for reflection in personal study. The author has recorded a series of video introductions to help make this volume suited for small group study.

As with the previous volumes, you can trust this book to provide carefully researched biblical evidence for holiness, and as such it is a valued new addition to the Word Aflame Press collection and now for your library as well.

Session 1

1

A Call to Holiness

"Follow peace with all men, and holiness, without which no man shall see the Lord" (Hebrews 12:14).

The Bible calls followers of Christ to a life of holiness and teaches its necessity. "Pursue peace with all people, and holiness, without which no one will see the Lord" (Hebrews 12:14, NKJV). The work of salvation begins with regeneration, or the new birth; continues with sanctification, a process of progressively becoming more like Christ in this life; and concludes with glorification, or resurrection with an immortal body and sinless perfection. Just as we must be born again to see the kingdom of God, so we must pursue holiness, or sanctification, in order to see the Lord. Holiness is not an option: it is a command to be implemented in all aspects of our lives. "As He who called you is holy, you also be holy in all your conduct, because it is written, 'Be holy, for I am holy'" (I Peter 1:15-16, NKJV). We obey this command in order to please God, for we belong to Him; to communicate Christ to others; and to benefit ourselves, both now and for eternity.

The new birth is the initial experience of salvation, but the work of salvation does not end there. God calls the Christian to a continued life of holiness. It is imperative for the born-again believer to experience the continuing work of sanctification, which comes by daily submission to the leadership and control of the Holy Spirit. Just as we must be born again to see the kingdom of God (John 3:3-5), so must we follow holiness or sanctification in order to see the Lord. The new birth will have no eternal value unless the born-again person continues to walk by faith and live after the new nature of the Spirit, allowing God to complete the work of salvation that began at the new birth.

This chapter presents in condensed form the basic principles of holiness.

Definition of Holiness

God is holy; holiness is an essential attribute of His nature. With respect to Him, it means absolute purity, and moral perfection. With respect to humankind, holiness means conformity to the character and will of God. We must be holy because God is holy (I Peter 1:15-16). It means thinking as God thinks, loving what He loves, hating what He hates, and acting as Christ would act.

Specifically, holiness consists of two components: (1) *separation* from sin and the world's values and (2) *dedication* to God and His will. "Wherefore come out from among them, and be ye separate, saith the Lord, and touch not the unclean thing: and I will receive you, and will be a Father unto you, and ye shall be my sons and daughters, saith the Lord Almighty. Having therefore these promises, dearly beloved, let us cleanse ourselves from all filthiness of the flesh and spirit, perfecting holiness in the fear of God" (II Corinthians 6:17-7:1). "I beseech you therefore, brethren, by the mercies of God, that ye present your bodies a living sacrifice, holy, acceptable unto God, which is your reasonable service. And be not conformed to this world: but be ye transformed by the renewing of your mind, that ye may prove what is that good, and acceptable, and perfect will of God" (Romans 12:1-2). The truth of Christ is "that ye put off, concerning your former conduct, the old man which grows corrupt according to the deceitful lusts, and be renewed in the spirit of your mind, and that you put on the new man which was created according to God, in righteousness and true holiness" (Ephesians 4:22-24, NKJV).

Holiness means to be like Christ. Instead of gratifying sinful desires, we put on Christ, letting Him be formed in us and adopting His mind (Romans 13:14; Galatians 4:19; Philippians 2:5). We judge decisions and actions by asking, What would Jesus do?

Holiness also means we cannot love this ungodly world system, identify with it, become attached to the things in it, or participate in its sinful pleasures and activities. "Know ye not that the friendship of the world is enmity with God? whosoever therefore will be a friend of the world is the enemy of God" (James 4:4). "Love not the world, neither the things that are in the world. If any man love the world, the love of the Father is not in him. For all that is in the world, the lust of the flesh, and the lust of the eyes, and the pride of life, is not of the Father, but is of the world" (I John 2:15-16). One important aspect of pure and undefiled religion is for a person to keep unspotted from the world (James 1:27).

Holiness involves both the inner person and the outer person (I Corinthians 6:19-20; I Thessalonians 5:23). We must perfect holiness by cleansing ourselves of filthiness both of the flesh and of the spirit (II Corinthians 7:1). For example, lustful thoughts are as sinful as an act of adultery (Matthew 5:27-28), and hatred is just as sinful as murder (I John 3:15). Holiness, then, includes attitudes, thoughts, and spiritual stewardship on the one hand and actions, appearance, and physical stewardship on the other. One without the other is insufficient. Inward holiness will produce outward holiness, but the outward appearance of holiness is worthless without inward holiness. For example, a modest spirit will produce modest dress, but modest dress is of little value if it conceals a lustful heart.

Holiness comes by faith, love, and walking after the Spirit. First, as with all aspects of salvation, we receive sanctification by grace through faith (Ephesians 2:8-9). Holiness is not a means of earning salvation but a result of salvation. We cannot manufacture our own holiness; we are partakers of God's holiness (Hebrews 12:10). Genuine faith results in obedience (Romans 1:5; 16:26; James 2:14-26). Thus, if we truly believe God, we will believe and obey His Word, which in turn will lead to the pursuit of holiness. If we deliberately and persistently disobey God's Word, then we are no longer walking in faith.

Second, if we truly love God, we will obey God's commandments (John 14:15, 23). Without love, all attempts to live for God are vain (I Corinthians 13:1-13). When we truly love God, we will actively hate evil (Psalm 97:10), and we will seek to become like our holy God. Love is stricter and more demanding than law, for love always goes further than duty. Love for God will cause us to draw closer to God than law will, both in attitudes and in disciplined living. Love will cause us to avoid everything that displeases God or hinders a closer walk with Him. Love rejects anything incompatible with godliness or not conducive to spiritual life, even though no law specifically labels it as sin. In this way, the principle of love leads to greater holiness than does the law of Moses or any other codification of rules. Love dominates all actions and all relationships.

Third, through the Spirit's guidance and power, we can overcome sin and live righteously (Romans 8:2-4; Galatians 5:16). We have freedom from sin's dominion—the power to choose not to sin (John 8:34-36; Romans 6:1-25). We will not continue to live in sin; indeed, when we act according to our new identity we cannot sin (I John 3:9). We still have the ability to sin and we still struggle with the inward nature of sin

(Galatians 5:16-17; I John 1:8; 2:1), but as long as we let the Holy Spirit lead us we will not sin.

Holiness is not an external law but an integral part of our new identity. The Spirit places God's moral law within us, not written on stone tablets but in our hearts (Hebrews 10:16). We do not merely follow an external list of rules, but we follow the Holy Spirit within us. We pursue holiness because that is who we are and want to be. We abstain from sin and worldliness because it is anathema to our new nature. We still struggle against the desires of the old nature, but it is an internal struggle. Nobody imposes rules on us; we restrict our flesh because we wish to follow the Spirit. We understand the beauty of holiness.

Following Holiness Requires Personal Effort

Holiness does not come automatically as we rest passively. Some teach that any attempt to live holy is "of the flesh," but they fail to understand that genuine faith always includes obedience and always produces good works. We must open our lives to the working of God's Spirit. We must actively implement the spiritual principles He places in us. We must resist the devil, subdue the sinful nature, discipline the flesh, and kill the deeds of the body.

Thus, the Bible teaches, "Reckon ye also yourselves to be dead indeed unto sin, but alive unto God through Jesus Christ our Lord. Let not sin therefore reign in your mortal body, that ye should obey it in the lusts thereof. Neither yield ye your members as instruments of unrighteousness unto sin: but yield yourselves unto God" (Romans 6:11-13). "Submit yourselves therefore to God. Resist the devil, and he will flee from you. Draw nigh to God, and he will draw nigh to you" (James 4:7-8). "Make every effort to be found spotless, blameless and at peace with him" (II Peter 3:14, NIV). Paul said,

"I run . . . I fight . . . I discipline my body and bring it into subjection" (I Corinthians, 9:26-27, NKJV). The Bible exhorts, "Let us cleanse ourselves. . . . Let us labour. . . . Let us lay aside every weight and . . . sin . . . let us run with patience" (II Corinthians 7:1; Hebrews 4:11; 12:1).

Philippians 2:12-13 sums it up well. "Work out your own salvation with fear and trembling. For it is God which worketh in you both to will and to do of his good pleasure." God gives believers both the desire and the power to live righteously. It is our responsibility to reverently and watchfully implement holiness in our lives, and this takes great personal effort and exertion. At the same time, God is actually the One working in us, and He provides both the desire and the power to live righteously. God's grace works *in* us, but we must work it *out*.

We wait for God to liberate us from struggles and temptations, when God expects us to use the power we already have in the Spirit and force the flesh to obey His Word. It is like the man who received a compliment on his garden: "You and God have really made this piece of land beautiful and productive!" The gardener replied, "You should have seen it when God had it by Himself."

A Daily Walk

If we live one day at a time, holiness becomes a possibility rather than an impossibility. We have the power of the Spirit and the promise that God will not allow us to be tempted beyond our capacity to bear it (I Corinthians 10:13). Therefore, unlike an unsaved person, we can say, "Regardless of the circumstances that will face me, I can live today without sinning." If we do sin that day, we can obtain forgiveness and begin the day anew. Jesus encouraged this type of thinking, for He told those whom He delivered, "Go, and sin no more" (John 5:14; 8:11). He also gave absolute perfection as the goal for which to strive: "Be ye therefore perfect, even as your Father which is in heaven is perfect" (Matthew 5:48).

A Continual Growth Process

The life of holiness is one of continual growth toward perfection or maturity (Matthew 5:48; II Corinthians 7:1; Philippians 3:12-16). Even though no one is absolutely perfect or holy as God is, we can all be perfect (mature) and holy in a relative sense (II Corinthians 7:1; Philippians 3:15; Colossians 1:28; 4:12). God will consider us holy if we live a repented life, have faith in Christ, live according to the knowledge of His Word, and strive to become progressively more Christ-like (Ephesians 4:13). He expects us to grow continually in grace and knowledge (Mark 4:26-29; II Peter 3:18), and to bear more and more spiritual fruit (John 15:1-8). If we do not become progressively more holy and Christ-like in thought, attitude, conduct, and lifestyle, something is wrong.

God evaluates us individually on the basis of where we have come from, what He has given us, and what our ability is (Matthew 13:23; 25:14-30). Two Christians can both be perfect in God's sight even though they have attained different levels of perfection in an absolute sense, just as two children at two different stages of growth can both be perfectly normal and healthy. We must not judge one another or compare one with another, but must be patient and tolerant of different levels of perfection, endeavoring to maintain the unity of the Spirit in the bond of peace (Matthew 7:1-5; II Corinthians 10:12; Ephesians 4:1-3).

None of us has yet attained the fullness of perfection. Paul wrote, "Not that I have already attained, or am already perfected; but I press on, that I may lay hold of that for which Christ Jesus has also laid hold of me. Brethren, I do not count myself to have apprehended; but one thing I do, forgetting those things which are behind and reaching forward to those things which are ahead, I press toward the goal for the prize of the upward call of God in Christ Jesus. Therefore let us, as many as are mature, have this mind; and if in anything you think otherwise, God will reveal even this to you. Nevertheless, to the degree that we have already attained, let us walk by the same rule, let us be of the same mind" (Philippians 3:12-16, NKJV).

We must be tolerant of different levels of maturity with respect to practical holiness even while we are careful to maintain the level which we have attained. We must let God be the judge of others. In particular, we should take great care not to condemn, intimidate, or offend visitors and new converts. Due to diversity of backgrounds, some people require more time than others to develop certain holiness convictions. It is better for new converts to develop solid scriptural convictions over a period of time than for them to conform immediately to every detail without understanding why.

God expects increasing production of spiritual fruit (John 15:1-8). Our goal is not to conform to the expectations of others but to follow the leading of God through His Word, Spirit, and church.

Three Teachers of Holiness

God has given three teachers of holiness. First, all holiness teachings come from the Bible, the inspired Word of God. Second, the Holy Spirit teaches us by internal promptings and convictions. Third, anointed preachers and teachers proclaim and apply the Word. God has given pastors for the oversight, care, and equipping of the church.

Some teachings are explicitly stated in Scripture. Others are practical applications of scriptural principles for our culture, time, and place. There may be some differences of opinion on exactly how to apply a principle or where to draw a line. Nevertheless, it is important for pastors to make practical applications, or else the principles will be neglected. Likewise, for our spiritual protection, for the unity of the body, and for a clear witness to the community, it is important for us to follow the teaching and admonition of godly pastors.

Self-Discipline

In particular, temperance is an important principle to implement in every aspect of daily living (I Corinthians 9:24-27). This means self-discipline, self-control, and moderation in all things. In the introduction to his book *The Disciplined Life*, Richard Taylor wrote, "Christians in a land of bulging supermarkets must discipline their appetites lest they fatten their bodies and stupefy their souls by habitual gourmandizing. They must beware the subtle, insidious tendency to judge the importance of themselves and others by the flashiness of their cars and the cut of their clothes. They must cease from careless spending and showy extravagance, not on the grounds of being unable to afford it, but on the grounds of principle. The alarming tide of moral casualties of recent years in both pulpit and pew is without question the result of that inner softness born of undisciplined, self-indulgent living."

Overcoming Sin: A Practical Approach

In the final analysis, holiness means to obey God's Word and to resist temptation to sin. As a practical matter, how is it possible to overcome sin on a daily basis?

First, we must pray. Prayer will draw us closer to God. Through prayer we commune with Christ and progressively absorb more of His mind and attitude. Paul prayed on many occasions that believers would develop spiritual strength and holiness of life (Ephesians 3:16; I Thessalonians 5:23). If prayers of another can avail to develop holiness in us, how much more can our own prayers do so!

In particular, it is important to pray in the Spirit. This means to reach a dimension of prayer in which the mind concentrates totally upon God and the human spirit unites with the Holy Spirit. This includes, but is not limited to, speaking in tongues (I Corinthians 14:14-15). When we pray in the Spirit, the Spirit Himself helps our weaknesses and intercedes through us to pray for what we truly need even though we do not know exactly how to pray (Romans 8:26).

Spiritual prayer is a powerful weapon of warfare against temptation (Ephesians 6:18). Jude admonished, "But ye, beloved, building up yourselves on your most holy faith, praying in the Holy Ghost, keep yourselves in the love of God" (Jude 20-21). Of course, it is not always possible to pray extensively at the moment of temptation. For this reason, it is important to have a consistent, strong prayer life at all times.

Second, we must engraft or implant the Word of God in our hearts so that we will obey His Word as a matter of course. "Therefore lay aside all filthiness and overflow of wickedness, and receive with meekness the implanted word, which is able to save your souls" (James 1:21, NKJV). We must absorb the Word until it becomes a very part of us. We can do this by hearing, reading, memorizing, and meditating upon the Word of God. "Blessed is the man that walketh not in the counsel of the ungodly, nor standeth in the way of sinners, nor sitteth in the seat of the scornful. But his delight is in the law of the Lord; and in his law doth he meditate day and night" (Psalm 1:1-2). "Thy word have I hid in mine heart, that I might not sin against thee. . . . I will delight myself in thy statutes: I will not forget thy word. . . . Thy word is a lamp unto my feet, and a light unto my path" (Psalm 119:11, 16, 105).

When temptation comes, we can recall the Word and speak it in our hearts. At the moment sin presents itself we must immediately begin to meditate on the Word before there is time for anything else. Jesus overcame temptation by quoting the Word (Matthew 4:1-11).

Third, we must personalize the truth of God's Word. We must realize both our personal ability and our personal responsibility to obey God and resist sin. We must recognize that we died to sin. In the time of temptation, we must recall the principles of Romans 6: *know, reckon, yield.* We should remind ourselves, "I do not have to do this. I am a free person. I have the power of the Spirit available to me. I can resist this temptation to sin."

Fourth, we must not give the sinful nature any opportunities. Instead, we must consciously avoid tempting or dangerous situations. We must not feed our fleshly desires by thinking, reading, watching, or indulging in things that would inflame those lusts. We must discipline the flesh and daily kill its desires. Basically, this means to cut off sinful thoughts and desires as they begin to develop. We must learn to think on good things (Philippians 4:8) and to make every thought obedient to Christ (II Corinthians 10:5). We must also learn to control all bodily appetites, for if we overindulge in physical appetites it will be more difficult to deny ourselves in other areas. Fasting is one good way to impose discipline on the physical body, not to punish it but to control it.

Finally, we must train ourselves to develop proper habits of Christian living instead of sinful habits. Developing good habits requires several things: repetition, commitment to consistency, diligence, refusal to make any exceptions, and refusal to get discouraged because of failure. We must learn to yield to God just as we formerly yielded to sin (Romans 6:13, 19). When we recognize and experience a scriptural prompting to do God's will, we must visualize and meditate upon the desired action, decide to do it, and then yield our bodily members to perform it.

Practical Applications Today

Holiness begins in the heart with attitudes and thoughts and extends to our way of life, behavior, appearance, and speech. We will briefly discuss some important areas in which biblical, and therefore universal and unchanging, principles of holiness apply.

Attitudes. (See Galatians 5:19-23; Ephesians 4:23-32.) The essence of holiness is to bear the fruit of the Spirit, which includes love, joy, peace, longsuffering, kindness, goodness, faithfulness, gentleness, and self-control. As Christians, we learn to forgive, obey authority, be thankful, not let anything offend us, and not be busybodies in others' lives. We put away evil attitudes such as hatred, malice, wrath, envy, jealousy, covetousness, bitterness, pride, prejudice, vengeance, strife, and discord. Holiness also includes justice and mercy in personal and social relationships.

Thoughts. (See Matthew 15:18-20; II Corinthians 10:5; Philippians 4:8.) We are what we think, and we become what we allow our minds to dwell upon. We are to think on true, noble, just, pure, lovely, commendable, virtuous, and praiseworthy things. We cast out temptations and evil thoughts, taking every thought captive to obey Christ.

The tongue. (See Colossians 4:6; James 1:26; 3:1-2; 4:11; 5:12.) We employ wholesome, gracious speech. Thus, we avoid tale bearing, backbiting, slander, sowing discord, swearing by oath, using the Lord's name in vain, pronouncing curses, reviling, lying, idle words, and suggestive, indecent, or obscene speech.

The eye. (See Psalm 101:2-3; 119:37; Matthew 6:22-23.) The eye is the gate of the soul and the primary source of input for the mind. We guard ourselves against reading or viewing things that are sensual, vulgar, immoral, or saturated with violence. Because of the widespread display of evil in modern media, we must be particularly mindful of the dangers associated with television programming, movies, and the Internet.

Appearance (adornment, dress, and hair). (See Deuteronomy 22:5; I Corinthians 11:1-16; I Timothy 2:8-10; I Peter 3:1-5.) The appearance reflects the inner self, both to God and to others. Worldly styles promote lust of the flesh, lust of the eyes, and pride of life, molding both wearer and society in ungodly ways. Biblical principles here include modesty, avoidance of personal ornamentation, moderation in cost, and distinction between male and female in dress and hair.

Stewardship of the body. (See I Corinthians 3:16-17; 6:12, 19-20.) The body is the temple of the Spirit, so we promote moderation and stewardship in diet, exercise, and rest. We do not use things that harm or defile the body, cause intoxication, or cause addiction.

Sanctity of marriage. (See I Corinthians 6:9-11; Colossians 3:5; Hebrews 13:4.) Marriage is the lifelong commitment of a man and a woman. Divorce is not God's plan but is a result of human sin. Sexual relationships are wholesome in marriage but sinful outside of marriage. We are to guard against lustful thoughts and actions.

Sanctity of human life. (See Exodus 20:13; Matthew 5:39, 44.) Humans were created in God's image; thus, we seek to avoid violence and bloodshed. Abortion and assisted suicide are wrongful takings of human life.

Honesty. (See Mark 10:19.) The Bible promotes integrity and rejects all dishonesty, including lying, theft, fraud, refusal to pay debts, extortion, bribery, and cheating.

Godly fellowship. (See Matthew 18:15-18; I Corinthians 5:9-6:8; 15:33.) We need wholesome fellowship, unity in the church, mutual accountability, and mutual submission. We should not associate closely with so-called believers who habitually indulge in sinful activities. We resolve internal disagreements within the church, not by secular lawsuits.

Worldly activities. (See I Thessalonians 5:22; Titus 3:3; I John 2:15.) We conduct activities in a wholesome atmosphere and seek to be a godly example in everything. With this in mind, we maturely regulate amusements, music, sports, and games.

Retaliation. The Bible expressly teaches against all forms of retaliation and vengeance (Matthew 5:38-48; Romans 12:17-21; I Peter 3:9). "Do not repay anyone evil for evil. . . . Do not take revenge, my friends, but leave room for God's wrath, for it is written: 'It is mine to avenge; I will repay,' says the Lord" (Romans 12:17, 19, NIV).

Greed and Materialism. Envy, jealousy, covetousness and greed are closely related evils. Covetousness and greed are basically synonymous terms, meaning an inordinate, unrestrained desire for wealth or possessions. This attitude is strongly condemned in both Testaments. "Thou shalt not covet" (Exodus 20:17). "Take heed, and beware of covetousness: for a man's life consisteth not in the abundance of the things which he possesseth" (Luke 12:15). Covetousness is idolatry (Colossians 3:5).

Envy and jealousy consist of a grudging of another's possessions or accomplishments together with a coveting of them. Jealousy often connotes an extreme desire to obtain or keep what we believe should be exclusively ours, while envy connotes an extreme desire to obtain what belongs to others.

The Bible's rejection of these attitudes stands as an indictment of the materialism of our age. Materialism—preoccupation with material possessions—causes us to become soft, lazy, and discontented with what we have. In turn, this makes us reluctant to live sacrificially for Christ's sake and highly susceptible to envy and jealousy.

The Bible's teaching on this subject is very relevant to our society, for by the standards of the rest of the world and of history we in North America are wealthy. "For we brought nothing, into this world, and it is certain we can carry nothing out. And having food and clothing, with these we shall be content. But those who desire to be rich fall into temptation and a snare, and into many foolish and harmful lusts which drown men in destruction and perdition. For the love of money is a root of all kinds of evil, for which some have strayed from the faith in their greediness, and pierced themselves through with many sorrows. But you, O man of God, flee these things and pursue righteousness, godliness, faith, love, patience, gentleness. . . . Command those who are rich in this present age not to be haughty, nor to trust in uncertain riches but in the living God, who gives us richly all things to enjoy. Let them do good, that they be rich in good works, ready to give, willing to share, storing up for themselves a good foundation for the time to come, that they may lay hold on eternal life" (I Timothy 6:7-11; 17-19, NKJV).

Prejudice. The Bible teaches that every human being is of equal worth in the sight of God. God is no respecter of persons (Acts 10:34; Romans 2:11). In Christ, there is no unequal treatment based on race, social class, or gender (Galatians 3:28). Paul admonished Timothy to perform his pastoral duties without prejudice, partiality, or favoritism (I Timothy 5:21). If we discriminate against one group and show partiality to another, then we violate God's Word. It is wrong to be prejudiced against someone because of race, social standing, lack of education, or poverty. "If ye have respect to persons, ye commit sin" (James 2:9). God "will surely reprove you if you secretly show partiality" (Job 13:10, NKJV).

Conclusion

God's moral law for us can be summed up in these words: Love God with all your being and love your fellow human as yourself (Matthew 22:36-40; Mark 12:28-31; Romans 13:8-10). In essence, holiness means to imitate Christ, to do what He would do. It means to be Christ-like.

The power to live a holy life is a gift from God, but it is our responsibility to implement holiness on a daily basis. We seek holiness out of love for God, not out of fear or legalism.

Holiness is an integral part of the salvation of the whole person from sin's power and effects. It is a joyful privilege; a part of abundant life; a blessing from God's grace; a glorious life of freedom and power. The life of holiness fulfills God's original intention and design for humanity. For the Spirit-filled believer who loves God, holiness is the normal—indeed the only—way to live.

Session 1

Discussion Questions

1. Without detailing the sin, tell about a time you were forgiven. Describe how you felt.

2. Why do you think we struggle so much with sin?

3. What is the connection between sin and holiness?

4. What is your personal definition of holiness?

5. Describe ways you personally safeguard against sin.

Session 2

2

The Dangers of Legalism

"A man is not justified by the works of the law, but by the faith of Jesus Christ" (Galatians 2:16).

Whenever pastors begin to teach practical holiness, they are somtimes accused of legalism. And, indeed, some of those who emphasize holiness do drift into legalism, doing more harm than good. In this chapter we address several key questions: What is legalism? What is wrong with legalism? What are the biblical alternatives to legalism? Is it possible to teach practical holiness and still avoid legalism? If so, how?

Legalism Defined

To ensure we do not drift into the dangerous waters of legalism we must understand what it is. In general, legalism means strict or excessive conformity to a legal code or set of rules. In a Christian context, legalism has two negative connotations: (1) attempting to base salvation on the performance of good works or on the strict observance of rules and regulations and (2) imposing rules on self and others that are not based on clear biblical teachings or principles. We are guilty of legalism if we imply that a person attains salvation by works or if we preach rules without principles.

Legalism Condemned

Legalism is detrimental and contradicts Christian principles. Jesus opposed the Jewish legalism of His day, particularly that of the Pharisees. These Jewish legalists believed that salvation rested in strict conformity to the law of Moses and the oral traditions they had built around it. Jesus rebuked this self-righteous attitude, the hypocrisy that accompanied it, and the human traditions that actually subverted the Word of God.

Paul pointed out that conformity to external law never meant anything unless the heart was right (Romans 2:17-29). Furthermore, the law of Moses could not and was never intended to impart salvation based on works (Romans 3:19-20; 8:3; Galatians 3:21-22). Rather, it served to teach us several important truths: the definition of sin, our own sinfulness, our lack of power to overcome sin, and our need of salvation (Romans 3:20; 5:20; 7:7-14). The law was a schoolmaster to bring us to Christ so that we would have faith in Him (Galatians 3:21-25). Throughout history, salvation has always been by faith, not by works. Abraham (before the law) and David (under the law) were saved by faith in God, not by good works or conformity to law (Romans 4).

The New Testament church contended for this doctrine of justification by faith against some Jewish Christians who still maintained legalistic concepts. These Judaizers taught that Gentile converts had to be circumcised and had to obey the Jewish law. The church convened its first general council to discuss this issue (Acts 15). At the conference, Peter said Gentile Christians should not have to obey the Jewish law, for God had already given them the Holy Ghost based on their faith alone. James pronounced the decision agreed upon by the church: Gentiles did not have to obey the law of Moses, except to abstain from food offered to idols, blood, things strangled, and fornication.

Paul strongly opposed legalism in general and the Judaizers in particular. He taught that we are justified by faith, not by observance of the law of Moses (Romans 3:20-28). We are saved by grace through faith, not by good works (Ephesians 2:8-9). The gospel of Christ has liberated us from the need to observe the ordinances of the Jewish law (Romans 7:6; Galatians 2:16-21). In fact, if we persist in seeking righteousness by works of the law, we frustrate the grace of God and make Christ's death vain (Galatians 2:21).

Specifically, Christ's death abolished the Jewish ceremonial law with its unclean foods and drinks, special festival days, and sabbaths. We do not have to follow ritualistic rules that forbid us even to touch certain unclean foods or other items. This kind of legalism may superficially seem to be wise and holy, but it has no power to restrain the lusts of the sinful nature. "Therefore let no one judge you in food, or in drink, or regarding a festival or a new moon or sabbaths, which are a shadow of things to come, but the substance is of Christ. . . . Therefore, if you died with Christ from the basic principles of the world, why, as though living in the world, do you subject yourselves to regulations 'Do not touch, do not taste, do not handle,' which all concern things which perish with the using—according to the commandments and doctrines of men? These things indeed have an appearance of wisdom in self-imposed religion, false humility, and neglect of the body, but are of no value against the indulgence of the flesh" (Colossians 2:16-17, 20-23, NKJV).

In short, legalism is an insufficient motivation to live for God. It will not bring salvation, nor will it produce true holiness. Let us investigate in detail the many inadequacies and dangers of legalism.

Self-Righteous Reliance on Works for Salvation

Legalism actually teaches salvation by human works instead of God's grace. Legalists will attempt to rely on their own human efforts instead of the power of the Holy Ghost. This can lead to pride, self-righteousness, and self-deception if legalists think they are actually saving themselves. On the other hand, it can lead to frustration, lack of assurance of salvation, fear, despair, and backsliding if legalists realize their inability to manufacture their own righteousness and to live by strict adherence to rules.

The Bible does stress the importance of good works as the inevitable result of saving grace and saving faith (Ephesians 2:10; Titus 2:11-12; 3:8; James 2:14-26). We must understand, however, that faith produces works, not vice versa. We do not get good to get God; we get God to get good. We do not work toward salvation; we work from salvation. We do not live holy in order to earn salvation; we live holy because we have salvation. We manifest continuing faith in God by a life of submission to Him and obedience to His Word.

A failure to manifest holiness, good works, and obedience indicates either a lack of genuine faith from the beginning or a loss of genuine faith. It indicates either failure to receive salvation initially or subsequent rejection of God's continuing work of salvation. If people continue in this condition, they will not be saved when Christ comes for them, but in no way does this imply that they can or must earn salvation by works. The root problem is not failure to produce works, but failure to maintain total faith in God and His Word.

Holiness comes by grace through faith as we submit to the sanctifying work of the Spirit in our lives. If we fail to submit, we reject God's grace and salvation. However, legalism actually sidesteps grace, faith, and the Spirit. It tries to produce holiness by human efforts alone and to purchase salvation by that human "holiness."

Failure to Develop Inward Holiness

As the preceding discussion indicates, legalism cannot produce inward holiness. No amount of legislating, keeping, or enforcing law will impart true holiness, for that can only come by the Holy Spirit. Legalism places utmost importance upon an outward show of holiness, while neglecting and ignoring the development of inward holiness (which, of course, will cause holiness to be exhibited outwardly). In the sight of humans, legalists may seem holy, but in the sight of God they are lacking. Even though legalists may be very strict in holiness teaching, they actually fail to develop holiness in their own lives and in the lives of those who follow them.

Failure to Develop a Mature Understanding of Principles

We understand the dangers of legalism, but how does a person become legalistic? In particular, legalists do not develop a mature conscience that can guide them to principled decisions in areas where their rules are silent. They walk the thin line between the world and the church. Sooner or later they will step into a gray area and perhaps go from there into sin. They often ignore new dangers that fall outside the scope of their rules. For example, perhaps they have grown up with a rule, "Thou shalt not attend movies," but they do not really understand the spiritual evils of the movies. When new technology introduces home movie systems, they may sense nothing wrong with showing the same movies at home. They may see nothing wrong with watching ungodly TV shows in public places, in a motel room, or on the Internet. Non-legalists will be quick to spot the danger because it violates their principles. They will abstain, not merely because someone forbade it, but because it is detrimental to and incompatible with their spiritual life.

Legalistic leaders constantly find themselves trying to invent and enforce new rules to cover new situations, because their followers do not know how to apply principles. This effort will always fail because it is impossible to invent enough rules to cover every possible circumstance.

Here are some extreme examples to illustrate how a legalist can actually miss the true teaching of God's Word even while supposedly following it literally. Jesus taught that if someone strikes me on the right cheek I should turn the other cheek. The legalist may say, "Ah, but Christ did not restrict my actions after that. After turning the other cheek, then I can get revenge." The legalist technically follows the letter of Christ's teaching as if it were a rule book, but misses the whole spirit of the passage, which teaches us not to react violently to insult and not to seek vengeance. In one place, Christ said we should forgive a brother seven times in one day, and in another place said we should forgive someone seventy times seven. The legalist may say, "I will forgive seven times in one day but not eight, or I will forgive 490 times but not 491." He or she misses the true teaching of complete, perfect, unlimited forgiveness.

Living by Minimum Requirements and Loopholes

Ironically, then, legalism frequently causes people to observe only the minimum of what they feel is absolutely required. Often they do this out of a desire to impress others. Their attitude is, "What are the minimum requirements of this church, of this pastor, and of salvation itself?" They have little desire to seek positive holiness, but define holiness in terms of the negative. They have little principles or conscience to guide them, and feel little restraint on indulging in non-Christian behavior if they can get away with it. They look for loopholes in their rules so they can justify whatever they want to do. They may justify participation in a questionable practice because no one has ever preached specifically against it or established a rule that definitely covered it.

In short, legalists treat Christianity as if it were a collection of rules like the US Tax Code. They feel no obligation other than what the rules specifically require. As long as they live by the letter of the law, they are free to exploit every doubtful situation or "loophole" without regard to God's will.

Hypocrisy and Inconsistency

Legalism results in negative side effects. First of all, it leads to hypocrisy. Since no set of rules can ever cover all situations, legalists usually end up doing as they please. If they cannot satisfy the desires of the flesh in one way, they usually manage to do so in another way. For example, some would never wear a necklace or an earring because of rules against them, but they will satisfy their desire for ornamentation by wearing extremely flashy rings and watches. Some will shun all jewelry but flaunt extravagant, outrageously expensive clothing. Others do not wear lipstick, but think nothing of wearing mascara or blush. They base their conduct only on specific rules of limited application. They are not truly concerned with upholding under all circumstances the biblical teachings against ornamentation, vanity, immodesty, and costly array.

Likewise, legalists may strongly condemn drinking but be oblivious to their own gluttony. They may avoid dirty movies but delight in dirty jokes. They may abhor idolatry but be a slave to materialism. Pursuing holiness with sincerity keeps us from these inconsistencies.

Human Rules

Legalism takes human rules and treats them as if they were the Word of God. It imposes rules that cannot be justified from the Bible. It goes much farther than the biblical text will warrant.

The Christian must limit himself to the Bible in establishing guidelines for conduct. All teachings must be taken either from a specific biblical injunction or from a valid application of biblical principles. For example, the Bible specifically describes drunkenness as sin, so we can and we must preach against drunkenness. In addition, the underlying biblical principle is that all intoxication is wrong; therefore we can preach against marijuana even though the Bible does not mention that drug by name. However, legalism goes beyond either biblical statements or principles, and establishes rules that originate in the mind of humans.

Misapplication of Principles

Legalists often take guidelines that once made some sense under certain circumstances and blindly misapply them to different circumstances. Without understanding the scriptural principle behind a certain guideline, they transplant it to a situation where it is unnecessary and inappropriate.

This causes confusion when someone tries to understand the system rationally or scripturally. For example, sometimes holiness people do not attend certain places of amusement in their community because of the worldly atmosphere, the type of people that attend them, and the type of ungodly activities associated with them. The legalist enshrines this as a rule: "Thou shalt not participate in this amusement." The non-legalist recognizes this as a practical application of important scriptural principles: "Abstain from the appearance of evil, love not the world nor the things of the world, avoid worldly pleasures, and avoid fellowship with unrighteousness." However, we should not look legalistically at the particular amusement in itself but whether participation is worldly or not in a given situation. We should understand the reason for the guideline. The amusement itself could be harmless or wholesome in a different setting.

Difficulty in Maintaining the System

It is extremely difficult to maintain a legalistic system. First, it is simply impossible for someone to abide by all the rules. Legalists will always fail. Either they will become hypocrites, condemning others but excusing themselves, or they will live under continual guilt and fear.

Furthermore, those who follow a legalistic leader will eventually begin to doubt the validity of the system because of its harsh and arbitrary rules. As children grow up in the system they begin to question the rules. When new converts enter the system they often accept everything uncritically, but sooner or later they, too, begin to analyze the rules.

If a church is founded on true scriptural principles, it will withstand scrutiny of its teachings. Legalists, however, usually give no justification for their human rules except tradition and authority. "This is what our church believes, and you must obey the church. This is what the pastor teaches, and you must obey the pastor." This kind of teaching will not be successful in developing true holiness.

Particularly in our questioning age, it simply does not work. People today are more sophisticated and educated than ever before. There is a greater willingness to challenge tradition and authority. Autocratic methods that people sometimes accepted in the past are less and less effective today.

Judgmental and Condemnatory Attitude

Finally, legalism fosters a judgmental, condemnatory attitude towards others. Legalists tend to pigeonhole everyone and then make their disapproval obvious to those found wanting. Legalistic church members often develop a harsh, intolerant, defensive attitude towards those who do not conform exactly to their rules, even towards visitors and new converts.

Even if someone is living in violation of God's Word, the Bible forbids the individual Christian to judge or condemn. Jesus said, "Judge not, that ye be not judged" (Matthew 7:1). We must simply present the Word of God without setting ourselves up as judges over someone else. Christ did not come to condemn the people of the world, for they are already condemned by their sin, but He came to offer salvation (John 3:17; 8:11). Likewise, the church's business is to offer salvation to all. We must let the Word and the Spirit bring conviction, and let God be the final judge.

Once, a long-haired man visited a certain church. He received so many stares and disapproving expressions that he felt very uncomfortable. Because of that experience, he vowed never to return again. This is a sad example of legalistic condemnation. The church does not have to *approve* of everything about a visitor, but it should *accept* the visitor for what he is and love him unconditionally. After all, that is how Christ treated sinners while on earth and how He treats everyone today.

In one church a new convert heard a minister proclaim, "It is a sin for a man to have hair on his ears." The new convert, whose hair covered his ears, decided that this church was a cult and resolved never to return again. Of course, the Bible does teach men to have short hair. A reasonable application of that principle in our day would result in cutting the hair above the ear and collar. Furthermore, the new convert should not have allowed anything to offend him. However, it seems to be legalistic overkill to state that a man will go to Hell if his hair touches his ear. We simply cannot find Scripture to support this statement. In any event, it serves no useful purpose to present this view in a harsh way to someone who does not have the spiritual maturity to evaluate it properly. It is the responsibility of the mature saint not to place a stumbling block in the path of others.

Improper Alternatives to Legalism

As mature Christians in a loving relationship with Jesus Christ, we want to avoid legalism, but what is the proper way to do so? Many people who see the dangers of legalism reject it, but in the process they sometimes discard practical holiness altogether. Frequently what happens is this: one generation discovers a life-changing relationship with God and embraces scriptural holiness. They rearrange their entire lifestyle around the concepts of separation from the world and dedication to God, and they pass this new-found lifestyle to the next generation. Somewhere in the process of transmission to future generations, legalistic tendencies creep in. What began as joyous submission to the will of God becomes a codified set of rules and regulations, which are justified on the basis of tradition and ritual.

Finally, one generation rebels against this cold, dry system and begins to question its values. Sometimes they fail to realize that many good and precious truths have been handed to them, albeit in the wrong way; they have been taught many right things for the wrong reasons. When they rightfully reject legalism, they also discard true holiness principles and valid practical applications. They throw the baby out with the bath water.

In such a case, the preceding generation is to blame for making the truth vulnerable by their nonbiblical approach in teaching it. On the other hand, the new generation is to blame for not studying these issues prayerfully and for not developing a genuine love for truth at all costs. They see legalistic tendencies they rightfully reject, but they use the occasion as an excuse to disregard any holiness standards and to indulge in the desires of the flesh. The root problem on both sides is a failure to commit quality time in serious, prayerful study of the Word of God.

Some suppose that we must abandon holiness teaching in order to have revival. However, we should never sacrifice quality in favor of quantity. In fact, the more we emphasize and implement the Word of God the more we will have true, apostolic revival. A church does not have to be legalistic to emphasize holiness. Nor does a church have to go to the opposite extreme of worldliness in order to grow. A conservative, holiness church can have revival. Indeed, most of our great revival churches strongly advocate holiness of life on a practical level.

In short, many suppose that the proper alternative to legalism is antinomianism (no law), license (freedom without responsibility), or libertinism (no moral restraints). They insist they can have inward holiness without any guidelines as to outward appearance and conduct. However, this attitude totally contradicts God's Word. True holiness is not freedom to act and look like the world, but freedom from conformity to the world. Intellectual freedom is not freedom from truth, but freedom to know and submit to truth. There can be no real freedom outside truth. "Ye shall know the truth, and the truth shall make you free" (John 8:32). Genuine spiritual freedom is not freedom to commit sin, but freedom from the bondage to sin.

The Importance of Moral Law

We must reject legalism as inadequate to bring about true holiness, but we must not reject God's moral law or the necessity of obedience to God's Word. God has always had law; He has always had specific commands that people must obey. Even in the age of innocence in the Garden of Eden He gave Adam and Eve a specific prohibition. God's moral nature never changes, and therefore neither does His moral law.

He has progressively revealed more of His moral law from Old Testament to New Testament times, but He has never abolished moral law. Jesus Himself told us that law or commandments would continue to exist in the New Testament church. "If ye love me, keep my commandments. . . . If a man love me, he will keep my words" (John 14:15, 23). He commissioned His disciples to teach all converts "to observe all things whatsoever I have commanded you" (Matthew 28:20).

Jesus did not come to destroy the law but to fulfill it (Matthew 5:17). When He opposed the Jewish legalism of His day, He indicated that true holiness would be even more demanding spiritually. "Except your righteousness shall exceed the righteousness of the scribes and Pharisees, ye shall in no case enter into the kingdom of heaven" (Matthew 5:20). He recognized that in most cases the Pharisees taught correct doctrine. He did not reject their teachings as much as he rejected their attitude and their inconsistent conduct. He told the people, "The scribes and the Pharisees sit in Moses' seat: All therefore whatsoever they bid you observe, that observe and do; but do not ye after their works: for they say, and do not" (Matthew 23:2-3).

The Pharisees were such sticklers for the law that they paid tithes even on small herbs, which grew in gardens. Jesus rebuked them for their attention to detail while disregarding more important things spiritually. Some today would say such attention to petty detail does not matter, but it only matters that motives and intentions be pure. However, Jesus did not rebuke the scrupulous tithe paying, but in fact commended it. He endorsed obedience to God's Word in both the seemingly insignificant details and in the larger principles (Matthew 23:23).

The doctrine of justification by faith does not destroy the principle of law but rather establishes it (Romans 3:31), for we do not need justification if there is no law to condemn us. God's laws are written in the believer's heart (Hebrews 10:16). The Spirit enables us to fulfill the righteousness that the law taught but could not produce (Romans 8:4).

As we have seen, Paul rejected ritualistic laws that forbade Christians to touch, taste, or handle foods regarded as ceremonially unclean (Colossians 2:14-23). Some today use this teaching to reject all moral guidelines and all restraints on worldly conduct. However, Paul also wrote, "Touch not the unclean thing" (II Corinthians 6:17). Paul did not contradict himself.

Christians today should still abstain from immoral, ungodly, worldly things. The ceremonial law has been abolished, but there are still many activities in this world that Christians must avoid as morally or spiritually unclean. Paul even compared the Christian life to a game with certain rules that must be obeyed to obtain victory: "And also if anyone competes in athletics, he is not crowned unless he competes according to the rules" (II Timothy 2:5, NKJV).

God still has many specific, practical guidelines as to what His people should and should not do. If we followed the definition of legalism that some use, Christ's Sermon on the Mount and many portions of Paul's epistles would be legalistic.

Some think our practical application of moral law is too restrictive. Moral law is indeed a restricting force, but that does not make it bad. The sinful nature needs a restraint upon its desires. The spiritual man needs protection against the evils of the world. Railroad tracks keep the train on course; without them the train would go nowhere. Gravity binds us to the earth; without it we would drift off into our own little world and die. Gravity keeps the earth allied with the sun; without it the earth would fly off on its own separate path without the life-sustaining light, heat, and energy that the sun provides.

The banks of a river define it and channel it. If the banks were moved farther apart without increasing the volume of water, the river would lose force and velocity. If the banks were eliminated, the river would dissipate its strength without arriving at its destination. It would lose its identity as a river. Likewise, holiness teachings do not force hardship on us, but bind us closely to a holy God who is our source of life and strength. They preserve our identity, channel our spiritual energy, provide direction, and enhance our spiritual strength, so that we can arrive at our final destination safely.

The fence around a garden does not serve to curb the freedom of the garden but to preserve its freedom. The fence protects the garden from external encroachment that would bring damage or destruction. In like manner, holiness teachings do not curb our freedom in Christ but protect us from evils that would destroy our freedom.

In rejecting legalism, then, we must be careful not to reject moral law or practical applications of moral law. We must still uphold specific biblical teachings as well as valid application of biblical principles to situations in modern society. We must not allow either the legalistic teachings of some or the "anti-law" teachings of others to deflect us from the path of holiness.

Conclusion

Our salvation and our holiness rest in Christ and the working of His Spirit, not in our own goodness. His Spirit produces holiness, both internally and externally, as we discipline ourselves, submit to Him, and obey Him.

We have principles to guide our conduct under all circumstances. We should not seek minimum requirements, but the application of principles to every situation, new or old. We must not be hypocritical, but should strive to live consistently by biblical principles, which are not made irrelevant by changes of culture, time, or geography.

Correct principles carry their own authority with them since they stem from the Word of God. We must not be judgmental of others because we recognize that our holiness comes from God and not from any goodness inherent within ourselves. We should not be condemnatory of others because our lives must be dominated by love.

Faith and love make us more concerned with leading sinners to salvation than changing their conduct. When they are born again, they will receive the desire and power to change, making it unnecessary to use harsh, dictatorial methods to teach them. Our reliance will be upon the power of the Word, the Spirit, and personal example. Instead of instantly imposing rules on new converts, we should exercise love, patience, and tolerance to let them mature at an individual rate of growth. We must preach that holiness results from salvation and that biblical principles form the base of all practical guidelines. Practical holiness is indeed scriptural, and a sincere convert will see this as he or she matures.

In conclusion, we can reject legalism and still emphasize practical holiness. This will be done when we place total faith in Jesus Christ, let our lives be dominated by love for Him, sincerely seek to obey the teachings of the Word of God, live in submission to the indwelling Holy Spirit, and make the personal effort required to implement holiness principles in our lives.

3

Christian Liberty

"For, brethren, ye have been called unto liberty; only use not liberty for an occasion to the flesh, but by love serve one another" (Galatians 5:13).

Biblical Christianity is not a life of drudgery but a life of liberty. Unfortunately, some people use this concept to justify their rejection of practical holiness teachings. Some discard many important aspects of moral law under this guise. Chapter 2 has shown that rejection of legalism does not nullify moral law, nor does it justify libertinism. This chapter discusses the biblical meaning of liberty in Christ and demonstrates that Christian liberty does not eliminate the need for personal holiness.

Freedom from Sin

First and foremost, Christian liberty means we are no longer under bondage to sin. Before our conversion we were at the mercy of the sinful nature and could not help but sin. If we seemingly conquered sin in one area, it would reassert its position in another aspect of our lives.

Through the Holy Spirit we now have power over sin—power not to sin. We can freely choose to sin or not to sin. Of course, as Christians we must choose not to sin. If we abuse our liberty and choose to live in sin again, we will surrender our new-found freedom. When a prisoner receives freedom, he has liberty to rejoin society; he is not given the liberty to return to jail each day. Likewise, we receive freedom from sin in order to have fellowship with God, not to return to the slavery of sin. For the first time, we are free to obey God and to become His servants (Romans 6:14-20, 22).

A person will either serve good or evil, God or Satan. He or she will either receive eternal life or death. There is no middle ground in which a person can live his or her own life without choosing either alternative.

Christian liberty cannot mean Christians are free to do as they please without reference to the will of God. By rejecting the will of God, they automatically choose the world, sin, and Satan. To be freed from the will of God automatically means submission to the dominion of sin. To be freed from sin automatically means submission to the will of God. By definition, to exercise Christian liberty means to break free from sin's bondage, to obey and serve God, which in turn means to serve "righteousness unto holiness" and to bear "fruit unto holiness."

Freedom from the Law

Christian liberty also means freedom from the law. As we discussed in Chapter 2 and in the preceding section, Christian liberty cannot mean that moral law has been abolished. Rather, it means that we have been freed from the law of the Old Testament in at least four specific ways: we are free from (1) the penalty of the law, (2) the attempt to fulfill the law by human effort alone, (3) the destructive power of the law that arises from human abuse of it, and (4) the ceremonial law.

First, we are freed from the penalty and condemnation of the law. The law condemned us to death, but when we apply Christ's atonement to our lives we are pardoned: "Christ hath redeemed us from the curse of the law" (Galatians 3:13). The law has no more power to condemn us when we are in Christ.

Second, we are freed from the attempt to fulfill the law through human effort alone. Of course, God never meant for the law to bring righteousness in itself; salvation has never been by works, but always by grace through faith (Ephesians 2:8-9), both before and during the law (Romans 4:1-12). God gave the law to define sin, to prove our utter sinfulness, to prove our need of God's grace, and to point us to Christ (Romans 3:20; 5:20; 7:7; Galatians 3:24).

In order to fulfill these purposes, God subjected people to the law, even though they did not have power to fulfill the law. God's people were actually under bondage to the law, just as a child is treated like a servant (slave) under tutors (guardians) and governors (administrators) until he or she reaches maturity (Galatians 4:1-11, 21-31).

Godly people in the Old Testament did not have the full power of the Holy Ghost available to them to overcome sin on a daily basis (Romans 8:3-4; Hebrews 8:7-13; I Peter 1:10-12). They were never able to live up to the law because they had to rely on weak, sinful flesh. They were saved by faith expressed in obedience to God's plan for that day; they attempted to fulfill the law and offered sacrifices continually to atone for their failures.

The gospel of Christ has delivered us from this bondage to the law. By faith in Christ, we receive the righteousness of Christ without the deeds of the law (Romans 3:28). Through the Holy Spirit, we can fulfill all the righteousness that the law demanded but could not impart. God counts us righteous (justifies us) through faith in Christ and progressively makes us righteous (sanctifies us) as we submit to and cooperate with His indwelling Spirit. Rather than being bound to an externally imposed law, we receive the moral law of God in our hearts as part of the regenerated nature (Romans 7:5-6; 8:1-4; Galatians 3:24-25; 5:18-23).

Third, we are freed from the destructive power of the law caused by human abuse of it. Many Jews at the time of Christ falsely believed they could obtain righteousness merely by the works of the law (Romans 9:31-10:4). This was a gross distortion of God's original purpose for giving the law. The law, which was good in itself, actually became a harmful force because they relied on it for salvation and so rejected Christ. Paul attacked this legalistic thinking in his day. Acts 15, Romans, and Galatians refute this doctrine as taught by some Jewish Christians.

Finally, we are specifically freed from the ceremonial law of the Old Testament (Mark 7:15; Galatians 3:24-25; 4:9-11, 21-31). God used the ceremonial law—including blood sacrifices, dietary laws, circumcision, sabbaths, and feasts—as types and foreshadowings of truth to be found in Christ and His gospel. Now that we have the substance (antitype) we no longer need the shadow (type). "When you were dead in your sins and in the uncircumcision of your sinful nature, God made you alive with Christ. He forgave us at. our sins, having canceled the written code, with its regulations, that was against us and that stood opposed to us; he took it away, nailing it to the cross. . . . Therefore do not let anyone judge you by what you eat or drink, or with regard to a religious festival, a New Moon celebration or a Sabbath day. These are a shadow of the things that were to come; the reality, however, is found in Christ" (Colossians 2:13-14, 16-17, NIV). Thus, the New Testament church refused to impose the Jewish law upon Gentile Christians (Acts 15).

Freedom in Non-Moral Matters

True to the principle of freedom from ceremonial law, Christians have liberty of action in non-moral matters. In general, Christians are free to participate in any activity or prac-

Christian Liberty

tice that does not violate biblical morality. They have freedom to follow individual judgment, desire, and conscience in areas where the Bible is silent.

Romans 14 gives guidelines for situations in which consciences differ. This chapter deals with morally indifferent issues, so we must be careful to apply its teachings within that context. The first controversial issue Paul addressed was the eating of meat. This could refer to vegetarianism, eating meat possibly offered to idols, or eating meat classified as unclean under Jewish law. Secondly, Paul discussed the proper observance of certain days, such as sabbaths and other Jewish holy days. Later in the chapter, Paul mentioned the drinking of wine (any juice from the grape). This, too, involved Jewish law, for juice from the grape could be ceremonially unclean (Daniel 1:8-16) or forbidden by a Nazarite vow (Numbers 6:3).

In each of these cases, the New Testament nowhere prohibits the questioned conduct, but in fact expressly forbids anyone to establish rules against it (Acts 15:19-29; Colossians 2:16; I Timothy 4:1-5). This chapter does not deal with morally objectionable practices or practices condemned by the Word of God.

With respect to these morally neutral issues, Paul presented several important guidelines: (1) We must not judge others, but must avoid controversies over these issues. The one who participates should not despise or ridicule the one who abstains. The one who abstains should not condemn the one who participates. (2) Everyone should have convictions and should follow them. If participators have faith in their liberty, they should keep it to themselves; if they have doubts, they should stop. Abstainers should continue to abstain if they have any doubts at all. (3) Whatever we do should be done unto the Lord, that is, with the conviction that we are obeying and glorifying the Lord in everything. In all things we must acknowledge the lordship of Christ. (4) In no case should we allow our exercise of Christian liberty to put an obstacle in the path of another. Rather than judging others, we should judge ourselves so that our actions will not cause others to stumble. We should not let our liberty destroy others or the work of God, but in all things we should seek peace and edification.

Paul also explained the proper use of Christian liberty in his discussion of food offered to idols (I Corinthians 8:1-13; 10:23-33). Since an idol is nothing, there is nothing inherently immoral or dangerous about eating food that someone had offered to an idol. However, if others saw a Christian eating food offered to idols, they probably would interpret it as endorsing or condoning idol worship. For their sakes, therefore, Paul told the Corinthians not to eat food they knew was offered to idols.

What if Christians buy food in the market or eat food at someone else's house? There is no need to worry about whether it has previously been offered to idols or not. For the sake of an onlooker's conscience, they should innocently eat the food without asking questions. In no case, however, can Christians insist upon liberty if their actions will harm others.

We Must Always Obey God's Word

Some people abuse the concept of Christian liberty in order to condone violation of holiness principles. In the last days ungodly people will "change the grace of our God into a license for immorality" (Jude 4, NIV). False teachers will appeal to lustful desires and promise liberty but will actually be under bondage to sin (II Peter 2:18-19). Some think they can continue to sin because they are no longer under the law but under grace. Their attitude is, "I can sin because I know God will forgive me." Paul rejected this philosophy emphatically: "God forbid!" (Romans 6:15).

As Chapter 2 discussed, God's moral law is still binding, and Christian liberty means freedom to submit to truth, not freedom from truth. Even though we have liberty, we must not use it to gratify the desires of the flesh. Christian liberty does not give us license to disobey God's moral law or the principles of God's Word. Paul explained, "You, my brothers, were called to be free. But do not use your freedom to indulge the sinful nature; rather, serve one another in love. . . . The acts of the sinful nature are obvious: sexual immorality, impurity and debauchery; idolatry and witchcraft; hatred, discord, jealousy, fits of rage, selfish ambition, dissensions, factions and envy; drunkenness, orgies, and the like. I warn you, as I did before, that those who live like this will not inherit the kingdom of God" (Galatians 5:13, 19-20, NIV).

God's Word also teaches submission to godly authority. Christian liberty does not eliminate our responsibility to follow His church and His leaders when they apply biblical principles of holiness to contemporary issues. "Obey them that have the rule over you, and submit yourselves: for they watch for your souls, as they that must give account, that they may do it with joy, and not with grief: for that is unprofitable for you" (Hebrews 13:17). The apostles and elders in Jerusalem wrote letters to Gentiles Christians specifying what was required of them: "For it seemed good to the Holy Ghost, and to us, to lay upon you no greater burden than these necessary things" (Acts 15:28).

Some people quote a few passages out of context in order to justify abandonment of all moral restraints. For example, Paul wrote, "I know, and am persuaded by the Lord Jesus, that there is nothing unclean of itself: but to him that esteemeth any thing to be unclean, to him it is unclean" (Romans 14:14). The context of this verse makes it clear that Paul was not referring to all activities but to non-moral issues. The immediate context shows that he specifically referred to the eating of certain types of food sometimes considered to be unclean (Romans 14:6, 15, 20). In fact, the NIV translates this clause as "I am fully convinced that no food is unclean in itself." This verse could not mean no activity is immoral in itself, for this would contradict all of Paul's practical teaching in chapters 12 and 13. Nor could it mean that all physical things are intended and fit for human consumption. Surely, Paul did not recommend for us to drink hemlock, bathe in poison ivy, smoke opium, or get drunk on alcohol!

In two other verses, Paul stated, "All things are lawful unto [for] me, but all things are not expedient" (I Corinthians 6:12; 10:23). Again, the context of each verse indicates that he was dealing with non-moral matters and specifically meant all foods are permissible to eat. First Corinthians 6:13 states, "Meats for the belly, and the belly for meats: but God shall destroy both it and them." The passage in I Corinthians 10 deals with the question of eating food offered to idols. Neither passage can be interpreted to mean that all activities are permissible, for I Corinthians 6:9-10 states, "Know ye not that the unrighteous shall not inherit the kingdom of God? Be not deceived: neither fornicators, nor idolaters, nor adulterers, nor effeminate, nor abusers of themselves with mankind, nor thieves, nor covetous, nor drunkards, nor revilers, nor extortioners, shall inherit the kingdom of God."

Guidelines for Proper Use of Christian Liberty

Our liberty does not permit us to indulge in fleshly desires, to commit sin, or to violate God's Word. We find other important guidelines for the proper exercise of Christian liberty, even with respect to non-moral matters.

(1) All exercise of liberty should be to the glory of God: (I Corinthians 10:31; Colossians 3:17).

(2) We should avoid anything detrimental to us, whether physically, mentally, or spiritually, even if it is not inherently sinful (I Corinthians 6:12). Many commentators believe Paul

quoted an expression the Corinthians used to justify questionable conduct and then commented upon it. Thus, the NIV translates, "'Everything is permissible for me'—but not everything is beneficial." I Corinthians 10:23 uses the word *edify:* "All things are lawful for me, but all things edify not."

(3) We must regulate our activities so that none of them controls us. We must not allow anything to dominate our will or rob us of too much energy, time, and money or interfere with our relationship with God. (I Corinthians 6:12).

(4) The Christian must never exercise liberty in a way that would harm others. (Romans 14:15-16, 20, NIV).

It is possible for something to be morally neutral in itself and yet violate one of these principles. Some things may be detrimental to one person and not to another, because of differences of personality, background, or experience before conversion. A certain situation may pose a great temptation for one person but not for another.

We must be careful to follow our own convictions even though others do not share them. Something could be wrong for one person even if not wrong for another person. If we violate a conviction solely because of pressure from others, we violate the faith principle in our life and may place ourselves in a damaging situation from which God is trying to protect us. We should not ridicule others' convictions because we may destroy a defense mechanism God has erected for them. At the same time, we should not try to impose our convictions on someone who may not need them as much as we do. Of course, this discussion applies only to situations not specifically covered by scriptural teachings.

Tolerance but Not Compromise

The concept of Christian liberty teaches us to be tolerant of the different personal convictions and preferences of fellow Christians. In no case can we compromise with sin. We must avoid the one extreme of legalism and the other extreme of condoning ungodly and immoral practices. A mature understanding of Christian liberty will show us that certain things are not sinful but yet are detrimental to us spiritually. Therefore, we can personally avoid them and even point out their dangers without necessarily condemning those who do not understand the dangers.

The legalist who does not understand Christian liberty is forced to pigeonhole everything in one of two categories: either a practice is sinful and will send one to Hell or it is not sinful and therefore perfectly permissible. However, it is scriptural to recognize that some things are not necessarily sinful in themselves but yet are not beneficial to Christian living.

Some things can be a "weight" or hindrance and yet not be sin (Hebrews 12:1). In such cases, a proper exercise of Christian liberty would cause us to avoid them. Yet, if some do not agree totally on this issue, we can still accept their status as a Christian. In this way, we can warn of the dangers of certain practices without being legalistic. This allows us to have fellowship with other believers without having to agree 100 percent on every personal conviction.

Legalism, Liberty, and Church Standards

How does our discussion of legalism and liberty affect the establishment of specific church standards for conduct? Certainly, the church must continue to teach against practices the Bible opposes. To do this effectively, ministers cannot merely parrot certain phrases but must explain the Bible's teachings and apply them to contemporary situations. The church must define clearly what it means to lie, to defraud, to dress immodestly, and so on. The writers of the epistles gave some very specific instructions with respect to situations in their day, and the church must do likewise today.

In some cases, the Bible presents a general principle but does not give detailed instructions for our culture. For example, it teaches men to have short hair but does not specify the precise length. It teaches women to dress modestly but does not describe a dress length. In such cases the church should reach a consensus as to the implementation of these principles. It must send forth a clear sound, presenting clear guidance to the believer and a clear witness to the unbeliever.

The church should not be chaotic but orderly, and its members should walk orderly and in unity (II Thessalonians 3:6-7). (See I Corinthians 14:8, 10 for an analogous situation.) If everyone did what was right in his or her own eyes without submitting to leadership, the result would be chaos and confusion (Judges 21:25). Some differences of opinion will exist, but since one Spirit has baptized us into one body we should be able to reach a reasonable position that all can uphold before the world.

This position should not be what we regard as the absolute minimum, but rather a moderate stance. It should be conservative, for we must live within biblically acceptable limits. (Only a legalist would insist on an absolute minimum. Others would rather be "extra" close to God rather than risk being too close to the world.)

Honest-hearted converts truly desire to know how to apply scriptural principles. They want practical direction from experienced, mature, spiritual leaders. A wise person appreciates counsel, instruction, correction, and reproof (Proverbs 11:14; 13:1; 17:10). True children of God seek godly leaders who will warn of danger and protect their souls (Hebrews 13:17). They will not despise or reject authority (II Peter 2:10; Jude 8), for God has established authority and government in the church to give specific guidance (I Corinthians 12:28; I Thessalonians 5:12-13; I Timothy 5:17; II Timothy 4:2).

Even in areas where we have Christian liberty, if the four principles we have discussed lead to one conclusion, then the church should teach that conclusion. Even though eating meat offered to idols fell within the scope of Christian liberty, Paul taught against it in all situations where it could be a stumbling block. Similarly, the council at Jerusalem did not hesitate to forbid this practice and to announce their decision as binding upon the whole church (Acts 15:28-29).

The church can uphold biblical standards of holiness and not be legalistic or violate Christian liberty. Standards can become legalistic, however, if we present them in the manner described in Chapter 2.

Legalism, Liberty, and Teaching

In particular, when we try to apply biblical principles to modern situations, we must be careful not to claim the same authority for our particular application that exists for the principle itself. If we maintain that every conceivable deviation from our particular application is a sin, we can fall into legalism.

For example, we believe quite strongly that it is not God's will for us to drink alcoholic beverages. Yet can we say the actual taste of alcohol is sinful? If so, it would be a sin to go to a restaurant and eat cherries jubilee or meat cooked in a wine sauce. It would be sinful to use vanilla extract. Those who use fermented wine at communion would be committing sin.

We also believe that most television programming is not conducive to godly living and that watching some movies can be sinful. Yet can we say the machine itself is evil or the act of watching the news is necessarily a sin? If so, glancing at a TV in a store display would be sinful. Watching a presidential address or a cultural event would be a sin.

The purpose of these examples is not to undermine solid holiness teaching, but to demonstrate the proper approach to holiness teaching. We do not have to take such arbitrary positions in order to maintain holy living. If we use a legalistic approach in teaching against certain practices, our rules will either be inconsistent or ridiculously harsh. We will alienate sincere, thinking people with unwarranted extremism. On the other hand, we can use a mature understanding of Christian liberty to approach holiness in a positive way. This approach will be moderate, temperate, and rational without surrendering important practical teachings. In fact, it will enhance those teachings and facilitate their acceptance.

For example, by properly applying Christian liberty we can teach that Christians should not drink alcoholic beverages. It violates scriptural guidelines for the proper exercise of Christian liberty: (1) It fails to give God glory in any way, but in fact it could bring a reproach. (2) It is physically, mentally, and spiritually damaging. (3) It has strong potential for getting mastery over us. (4) It is a stumbling block to others, particularly to members of our own family.

Conclusion

John Calvin defined Christian liberty as consisting of three things. First, we renounce the righteousness that comes by observing law and look solely to Christ for righteousness. Second, the conscience is freed from the yoke of the law and voluntarily obeys the will of God. Third, we have the free use of morally indifferent things. Calvin observed that Christian liberty is "perversely interpreted by some who use it as a cloak for their lust, and they may licentiously abuse the good gifts of God."

In summary, the Christian life is characterized by liberty. Through the gospel of Jesus Christ we receive freedom from sin, freedom from the law, and freedom to act as we will in non-moral matters. We follow "the law of liberty," which means freedom to do God's will and to obey His Word (James 1:25; 2:12).

In no case does Christian liberty give us license to commit sin, violate God's Word, or gratify the lusts of the flesh. Furthermore, our exercise of Christian liberty must always be regulated by four questions: (1) Can I glorify God in this activity? (2) Is this activity detrimental physically, mentally, or spiritually? (3) Can this activity gain mastery over me and bring me under its control? (4) Is this activity a stumbling block to another believer or to an unbeliever? These guidelines even extend to things morally neutral or innocent in themselves.

If the Bible condemns a practice either specifically or in principle, then we must obey. If the four basic guidelines for exercise of Christian liberty point to a certain course of action, then again we obey. If an issue is morally neutral and the four guidelines do not define a certain response, we apply the teaching of Romans 14. We must grant liberty to others and not treat our private convictions as gospel. We must not impose our tradition, preferences, or habits upon others and condemn them as sinners if they do not conform. The participator should not despise the abstainer and the abstainer should not condemn the participator, but everyone should avoid contention, seek peace, and seek to edify. No one should judge another in the matter, but each must be true to his or her own convictions.

When we implement the concept of Christian liberty, we will find that it does not detract from but rather it enhances holiness teaching. It is the biblical alternative to legalism. A mature understanding of our liberty in Christ will motivate us to live a holy life worthy of the freedom given to us. Christian liberty will lead to a life of greater holiness, because it enables us for the first time to submit voluntarily to the will of God. Liberated from the bondage of sin and the law, we freely choose to obey the Word of God.

Session 2

Discussion Questions

1. Why do you think a person might become legalistic?

2. How can we avoid our holiness turning into legalism?

3. Why is moral law important and what is its connection to holiness?

4. How can we say God is both absolute in His holiness and yet a God of love?

5. Paul described guidelines for Christian liberty concerning the eating of meat. What would be a modern-day example of a similar principle, and what would be the overarching guidelines for addressing the situation?

Session 3

4

The Christian Life

"The just shall live by faith" (Galatians 3:11).
"But the fruit of the Spirit is love, joy, peace, longsuffering, gentleness, goodness, faith, meekness, temperance" (Galatians 5:22-23).

Basic Concepts of Christian Living

When Christians talk about holiness, it is easy to emphasize rules, regulations, do's and don'ts. In a book of this kind it is difficult to be specific, plain, and honest without running the risk of seeming legalistic. This chapter attempts to put things in proper perspective by describing the basic nature of the Christian walk. The Christian life is one of faith and liberty, not one of legalism or drudgery. Instead of merely trying not to do wrong, we are trying to bear fruit pleasing to God. Simply put, we want to imitate Christ. This chapter will define the essence of the Christian experience: namely, that the Christian experience is one of personal freedom from sin and the law, that it is a life of personal consecration to God, and that we display holiness by imitating the life of Christ and by bearing the fruit of the Spirit.

The first reason for holiness is to please God, for His sake. He purchased us with His own blood, and we belong not to ourselves but to Him (I Corinthians 6:19-20; I Peter 1:18-19).

Therefore, we cannot live to ourselves, but we must live unto Christ (II Corinthians 5:15). The second reason for holiness is to communicate Christ to others. We attract and win others to Him by the example of our lives. The third reason for holiness is for our own benefit. The Christian life of holiness is the best plan for our lives. It will benefit us both now and in the life to come.

The Work of the Spirit

The Spirit baptizes us into the body of Christ (I Corinthians 12:13) and adopts us into the family of God (Romans 8:15-16). In other words, the Spirit gives us a new identity. We are transformed by the indwelling Spirit of Christ—Christ in us (Romans 8:9; Colossians 1:27). We put on the mind of Christ (I Corinthians 2:16; Philippians 2:5). Christ is formed in us (Galatians 4:19). The Spirit of God conforms us to the image of Christ (Romans 8:29). We are able to live holy lives by letting the mind, personality, and will of Jesus Christ supersede our own. Jesus lived on the earth for thirty-three years to give us an example to follow (I Peter 2:21-24). He died and rose again to defeat sin and death and to give us power to follow His example (Romans 8:3-4).

Holiness means letting the Spirit and personality of Christ shine through us. We want to display His Spirit. We want to please Him and be like Him. We want to live as He lived and do what He would do. We want to manifest the characteristics and traits of Jesus Christ. In this way we become living examples of Christianity. We become open letters from Christ to the world, written by the Spirit (II Corinthians 3:2-3). The good works that He produces in us will lead people to God, and they will glorify Him.

Christian Characteristics

What are the characteristics that Christians (Christ-like people) display? Galatians 5:22-23 gives us an excellent list, known as the fruit of the Spirit. If we have the Spirit in us, we will bear this fruit. While speaking in other tongues is the initial evidence of receiving the Holy Spirit, the abiding evidence that the Holy Spirit dwells in a life is the manifestation of the fruit of the Spirit. Paul listed nine aspects of spiritual fruit: love, joy, peace, longsuffering, gentleness, goodness, faith, meekness, and temperance. Peter listed eight qualities that will make us fruitful in Christ: faith, virtue, knowledge, temperance, patience, godliness, brotherly kindness, and charity (II Peter 1:5-10). Faith and temperance are repeated in both lists. Virtue and godliness are aspects of goodness, brotherly kindness and charity are aspects of love, and patience is similar to longsuffering. Peter also noted some characteristics of Christ for us to imitate (I Peter 2:21-24). The passage explains that Christ had no sin or guile (deceit) and describes His love, patience, temperance, and faith while suffering for our sins. This is the fruit God wants us to bear, and this is the fruit that will attract sinners to the gospel message.

Love is the most basic element of our Christian life. It is the only acceptable motivation for serving God. We are commanded to love our fellow Christians, to love our neighbors, and even to love our enemies. If we do not love our fellow humans, then we do not love God. If we love the world, then we do not love God. Love is the test of true Christianity.

If we understand what love really means, we can fulfill the Bible's teaching on holiness. For example, love one for another will eliminate jealousy, strife, talebearing, complaining, and bitterness. Love for God will eliminate worldliness and rebellion. On the other hand, if we do not love both God and people, then nothing will make us right in the sight of God. Correct doctrines and good works cannot take the place of love. The closer to God we become, the more love we will have.

Joy. As with the other aspects of spiritual fruit, we receive joy from the Holy Spirit. Our experience with God is "joy unspeakable and full of glory" (I Peter 1:8). We can have God's joy no matter what happens to us. This joy is different from what the world gives, for it is not dependent on circumstances. Regardless of external conditions, we can always rejoice in our salvation and in the God of our salvation (Luke 10:20; Habakkuk 3:17-18). Joy is a weapon and a source of strength. When discouragement comes, we can draw upon the joy of the Spirit. The way to overcome in time of trial is to "count it all joy when ye fall into divers temptations" (James 1:2). We can praise our way to victory.

How do we obtain joy in time of need? Our salvation itself is a source of joy. "Therefore with joy shall ye draw water out of the wells of salvation. And in that day shall ye say, Praise the LORD" (Isaiah 12:3-4). Psalms tells us about two other sources of joy. "They that sow in tears shall reap in joy" (Psalm 126:5). If we plant good seed with tears and prayers, we will reap good results with joy. "In thy presence is fulness of joy" (Psalm 16:11). When we draw close to God and enter into His presence, we have perfect joy. We can enter into His presence with singing, thanksgiving, and praise (Psalm 100).

Peace. We also have peace in the Holy Spirit—peace that passes all understanding and peace about which the world knows nothing (Romans 14:17; Philippians 4:7). No matter what happens, we can have inner peace. Jesus said, "Peace I leave with you, my peace I give unto you: not as the world giveth, give I unto you. Let not your heart be troubled, neither let it be afraid" (John 14:27).

Not only can we have peace of mind but also peace with others. In fact, God expects this of us. "Follow peace with all men" (Hebrews 12:14). Jesus said, "Blessed are the peacemakers"—those who make peace where there is no peace, those who bring peace to a troubled person or a troubled situation (Matthew 5:9).

How can we acquire and maintain peace in our lives? We will have perfect peace if we focus our minds on God and trust Him. "Thou wilt keep him in perfect peace, whose mind is stayed on thee: because he trusteth in thee" (Isaiah 26:3). We experience peace as we rejoice in the Lord, live in moderation (gentleness), lay aside anxiety, and make our requests known to God through prayer and supplication with thanksgiving (Philippians 4:4-7).

Longsuffering or patience is important in our Christian experience. Jesus said, "In your patience possess ye your souls" (Luke 21:19). We bear fruit with patience (Luke 8:15), we run our race with patience (Hebrews 12:1), and we obtain promises by faith and patience (Hebrews 6:12). "For ye have need of patience, that, after ye have done the will of God, ye might receive the promise" (Hebrews 10:36).

Longsuffering connotes patience or forbearance in relationships with people. Paul implored us to walk worthy of our calling, "with all lowliness and meekness, with longsuffering, forbearing one another in love; endeavouring to keep the unity of the Spirit in the bond of peace" (Ephesians 4:2-3). Longsuffering comes with meekness, love, a desire for unity, and a desire for peace. Patience comes by the trying of faith and by tribulation (Romans 5:3; James 1:3). If we let patience have its perfect work, we will have experience, hope, and everything else that we need (Romans 5:4; James 1:4).

Gentleness is not the same as weakness. To be gentle is to be courteous, mannerly, kind, patient, serene, and not harsh, violent, or rough. Jesus was gentle in dealing with people, yet He was firm and decisive when necessary. The Lord wants us to be gentle toward everyone (II Timothy 2:24). His gentleness will make us great (Psalm 18:35).

Goodness. This word includes righteousness, morality, virtue, and excellence. We must remember that "there is none good but one, that is, God" (Mark 10:18). Any good thing we have comes from Him (James 1:17). All our righteousness is as filthy rags in His sight (Isaiah 64:6); only the righteousness of Christ saves us. When we have faith in Jesus, we receive His righteousness (Romans 4:5-6). We are saved as we continue in God's goodness (Romans 11:22).

Faith. Not only do we need faith to be saved, but we need faith to continue our Christian walk. Without faith it is impossible to please God (Hebrews 11:6). Faith causes us to realize that all things work together for good to those who love God (Romans 8:28). Faith assures us God will never allow us to be tempted more than we can bear and that He will always provide a way of escape (I Corinthians 10:13). Faith results in answered prayer, supplied needs, and fulfilled promises. "And all things, whatsoever ye shall ask in prayer, believing, ye shall receive" (Matthew 21:22). This aspect of spiritual fruit involves faithfulness, which means being loyal, true, constant, and consistent.

How do we receive faith? God has given a measure of faith to everyone (Romans 12:3). Surely we have as much faith as a grain of mustard seed, and if we will exercise this much faith, nothing will be impossible (Matthew 17:20). We build faith primarily by hearing the preaching and teaching of God's Word and by reading the promises of God's Word (Romans 10:17). We can also increase our faith by hearing the testimonies of others and by drawing upon our own past experiences with God. Faith can also come in a critical moment as a supernatural gift of the Spirit (I Corinthians 12:9).

Meekness. To be meek means to be patient, mild, and not inclined to anger or resentment. It does not mean weakness or spinelessness. Meekness includes humility—a realization that we are nothing without God and that we must have His help. Meekness is an important quality for leaders to have. Moses was the meekest man in his day, and Jesus described Himself as meek and lowly. Jesus said that the meek would inherit the earth (Matthew 5:5). The Lord wants us to show meekness to everyone (Titus 3:2).

Here are some things the Bible says should be done with meekness: preaching the Word (II Corinthians 10:1), receiving the Word (James 1:21), helping and restoring an erring brother (Galatians 6:1), displaying wisdom (James 3:13), and adorning our lives (I Peter 3:4). Meekness is an attitude we must consciously develop in ourselves. It takes effort on our part. "Submit yourselves therefore to God. . . . Humble yourselves in the sight of the Lord" (James 4:7, 10).

Temperance encompasses self-restraint, self-control, and moderation. Any pleasure can become painful if carried to excess, and any good thing can be ruined by taking it to extremes. In I Corinthians 9:24-27 Paul illustrated the concept of temperance by a runner in a race. To win, runners must be "temperate in all things." They must have discipline and self-control. They must have a well-balanced training program and must be moderate in their activities. Likewise, Paul had discipline and control. He knew what his goal was, and he kept his body under subjection. Temperance or self-control is an attribute that we need to display at all times.

Church Meetings

At the first general conference of the church (Acts 15), an important, controversial issue was decided—namely, what practices of the Jewish law are mandatory for Gentile Christians. Delegates came to Jerusalem, where they met with the apostles and elders (pastors) there (verses 2-4). Both sides debated and disputed at great length, with the major views being fully represented (verse 7). Finally, they reached a decision, which everyone agreed to support. They sent letters to the various congregations informing them of this decision (15:23; 16:4).

We should notice that the leaders of the church worked together after the decision despite the sharp differences of opinion that had originally existed. They also worked together in sending letters of recommendation and collecting special offerings (Acts 18:27; II Corinthians 8:19). They loved each other, helped each other, and even rebuked each other when they saw the need. Paul rebuked Peter and others "when I saw that they walked not uprightly according to the truth of the gospel" (Galatians 2:14).

What took place in Acts 15 was a democratic discussion in which a strong majority of the elders formulated a decision under the influence of the Holy Spirit (verse 28). After this conference, the church united in support of the decision. Democracy does not mean doing whatever we choose and never listening to someone else, but it means following the majority on nonessential, nondoctrinal matters. When a majority makes a decision, we should accept the decision with a good attitude, without murmuring, complaining, or sowing discord.

If we have confidence in our leaders and fellow ministers, then it is easy to believe that God can influence a majority of them in the right direction. If we love our fellow believers, we can accede to the wishes of the majority. At the same time, the leaders must not have an attitude of pride that says, "I am the leader, so you do as I say." Ministers are not lords over God's heritage but examples to the flock (I Peter 5:3). All of us should manifest brotherly and sisterly love, "in honour preferring one another" (Romans 12:10).

What should a business meeting or a conference be like? The participants should not speak with anger, resentment, or bitterness. How can we act in this manner and at the same time inspire others? How can we exercise the ministry of reconciliation if we cannot get along with each other? A conference is a time to conduct business but also a time for fellowship, healing, renewal, and the outpouring of the Holy

Spirit. It should be a time for strengthening convictions and listening to others proclaim the message that we love. It is refreshing to hear someone else explain the truth in such a way that we can say, "This is what I believe, too." Conferences are times for mutual encouragement, not for talebearing, murmuring, complaining, or disputing.

In the business of the church, let us guard against a stubborn attitude. It should be a warning if we find ourselves saying, "Well, I'll just do it anyway"; "If they don't do it my way, I won't participate"; or "I don't need anyone to tell me what to do." Instead, the church should foster unity, respect, and collaboration as we each strive for holiness in all areas of Christian living.

The Roles of Men and Women

God created male and female and throughout Scripture attention is given to distinction of gender. Yet men and women can and should be able to interact as brothers and sisters in the Lord with peace and unity.

Historically societies have struggled with proper interaction as evidenced by the feminist movement in the Western world. Some things about the feminist movement are consistent with the Word of God, but some things are not. On the positive side, the Bible teaches that women and men are equal in importance and value. They are potentially equal in talent, intelligence, and spiritual gifts. There is no unequal treatment of male and female in Christ (Galatians 3:28). Throughout the Bible, God used women as prophetesses, judges, teachers, deaconesses, and laborers in the gospel. (See Judges 4:4; Isaiah 8:3; Acts 18:26; 21:9; Romans 16:1; Philippians 4:3.) Applying these principles to daily life, women and men deserve equal pay for equal performance of the same job.

At the same time, the roles of wife and husband are different, and so are the roles of mother and father. The Bible teaches mutual submission to one another, and it also teaches that the wife should follow the godly leadership of her own husband. (See Ephesians 5:21-22; Colossians 3:18; I Peter 3:1.) God has given the husband the primary responsibility of providing for his family and leading them in righteousness. Along with that responsibility comes the authority to fulfill this role.

The husband is to love his wife as Christ loves the church and to treat her kindly (Ephesians 5:25; Colossians 3:19). He is to honor and respect her; otherwise, his prayers will be hindered (I Peter 3:7).

The ancient Jewish rabbis pointed out that in the Genesis account the woman came from the side of the man, not from his head or his feet. Thus, they explained, she is not to lead him, nor is he to dominate her, but he should cherish her by his side. She is a helper comparable to and suitable for him; husband and wife complement each other (Genesis 2:18). A wife's first responsibility is to help her husband and care for her children. The Bible strongly advocates marriage and the home, while condemning extramarital sexual relationships, homosexuality, and lesbianism. (See chapter 11.)

Can any man assert authority over any woman? No. A man is the leader of his own home, and a woman should respect the leadership of her own husband. Beyond that, general principles of leadership and authority apply.

In the early church, women prayed and prophesied publicly (Acts 2:17; 21:9; I Corinthians 11:5; 14:31). However, they were not to interrupt a public assembly to ask questions—a privilege that men often had in those days (I Corinthians 14:34-35). In the New Testament, women functioned in leadership and ministry roles (Romans 16:1-12). However, they were not to usurp authority but fulfilled leadership and teaching roles under the authority of men (I Timothy 2:11-12).

In spiritual matters, a woman should follow the leadership of her husband as he follows the Lord. Even if he is not a Christian, she should acknowledge him as the leader of the family in order to win him to God (I Peter 3:1-2). On matters of personal conviction, doctrine, and spiritual experience, a woman must be true to her own individual beliefs since God ultimately will judge everyone on an individual basis.

Holiness As a Way of Life

In the final analysis, we can only give suggestions and advice based on prayer, biblical study, and experience. God gives each individual the privilege and responsibility to respond according to his or her own conscience. Of course, we are all responsible to obey the clear teachings of Scripture regardless of personal opinions and desires.

The Christian life is a personal relationship with God. It is a continual search for holiness as we draw close to God and become more like Him. If we will let His Spirit lead us and if we will cultivate the fruit of the Spirit, then the pursuit of holiness will not be difficult. It will be a joy and not a burden. It will be the way we want to live.

5

Christian Attitudes

"Let all bitterness, and wrath, and anger, and clamour, and evil speaking, be put away from you, with all malice: and be ye kind one to another, tenderhearted, forgiving one another, even as God for Christ's sake hath forgiven you" (Ephesians 4:31-32).

Cultivating a holy attitude is an important part of the Christian life. In fact attitudes are the most important elements of holiness. If we have the proper attitude toward God and our fellow humans, we will manifest holiness in all areas of life. If we do not have the right attitude, no amount of outward holiness will compensate for the lack of inward holiness in the sight of God. Wrong attitudes are the first signs of backsliding and are inevitable components of hypocrisy.

Love

Once again, we emphasize that love is the basic attitude that distinguishes true Christians from the world. We can sum up all the law and prophets in two commandments: Love God and love our fellow humans (Matthew 22:36-40; Mark 12:28-31; Luke 10:27). Love will cause us to keep God's commandments (John 14:15, 23). In fact, we demonstrate our love for God by how faithfully we obey His Word (I John 2:3-5).

Jesus commanded that we love one another even as He has loved us (John 15:12, 17). Love one to another is the ultimate test of true Christianity (John 13:34-35). If we do not love our brothers and sisters, then we do not love God (I John 4:20-21). Love is the fulfillment of the law (Leviticus 19:18; Romans 13:10; James 2:8). God calls Christians to extend love to every human being, even enemies (Matthew 5:43-48). Once again, this type of love is the ultimate proof of Christianity, for even sinners love those who love them in return (Matthew 5:46).

We cannot overemphasize the necessity of love as the basis for all actions and all relationships. Love never fails (I Corinthians 13:8). We will not fail God or each other if we let love have its perfect work. No activity or attribute is worth anything if love is not the underlying force and motivating factor (I Corinthians 13:1-3; Revelation 2:1-5). The preceding passages list the following things that are valueless without love: speaking in tongues, eloquence, prophecy, wisdom, knowledge, faith, sacrifice, philanthropy, works, labor, patience, right doctrine, right leadership, right fellowship, perseverance, and zeal for Jesus' name.

Let us apply these teachings about love to the subject of holiness. First, we should love God enough to do His perfect will. If we love Him as we should, we will want to be like Him as much as possible. We will try to avoid anything that is not like Him. We will want to please Him even in areas that from a human viewpoint might seem to be unnecessary or trivial. If we begin to question holiness teachings, we should check to see how deep our love for God really is.

Second, we should be on guard when any type of resentment or dislike arises in us toward another human being. We must retain a loving and forgiving attitude toward that person if we want to maintain our holiness and our Christianity. Love for others means we are patient, kind, not envious, not egotistical, not boastful, mannerly, not self-seeking, not easily provoked, slow to think evil of someone, and pleased only with what is good. Love bears all things, believes all things, hopes all things, and endures all things (I Corinthians 13:4-7). Our actions must be motivated by this kind of love for God and our fellow humans. Following holiness teachings for any other reason or without this love is worthless and will lead to hypocrisy.

Attitudes to Avoid

Having established the importance of right attitudes, let us examine some specific teachings concerning them. Ephesians 4:31, quoted at the beginning of this chapter, lists some dangerous attitudes that Christians must put away. If we allow these attitudes to remain in our lives, we will feed the flesh and starve our spiritual life.

Bitterness is something sharp, disagreeable, distasteful, harsh, severe, resentful, or vehement. This type of attitude produces piercing remarks and unpleasant language. It is never appropriate. Some people think they can put aside their spirituality and give vent to their bitterness, but they cannot do so if they want to be holy. Even when leaders issue necessary rebukes, they must not do so with personal bitterness or with sharp, disagreeable, harsh, severe words. There is a time for rebuke and exhortation but never with bitterness.

Wrath is violent anger, rage, or indignation; the word suggests a desire to avenge or punish. The flesh wants to get revenge, and it often does so by a display of harsh feelings or a cutting remark. We may disagree on certain issues, but we must not become resentful or vengeful. We may be perfectly correct in principle, but if we allow ourselves to become violently angry or wrathful then we are wrong. The same is true about the other wrong attitudes we are discussing. We cannot allow ourselves to be ungoverned, but we must learn to control our feelings. Instead of relying upon our own strength, we control wrath through prayer and seeking God.

It is especially disgraceful for a minister to become violently angry or resentful, even with regard to the work of the church. There is no way to explain this lack of control to followers. We must remember that "the wrath of man worketh not the righteousness of God" (James 1:20).

Anger is a feeling of extreme displeasure that usually results from injury or opposition. The word itself does not suggest a definite degree of intensity, nor does it necessarily require an outward manifestation. If anger is allowed to go uncontrolled, it usually manifests itself as a desire to lash out at someone or something. If controlled and used properly, anger may be constructive and even beneficial. For example, Jesus displayed anger against sin when He cleansed the Temple of thieves. Thus, anger itself is not sinful, but in many situations it can easily lead to sin.

What kind of anger is permissible and what is not? "Be ye angry, and sin not: let not the sun go down upon your wrath" (Ephesians 4:26). Anger that causes us to harm someone in word or deed is wrong. Anger that we carry in our heart and nurse into a grudge is also wrong. Anger without a cause is wrong (Matthew 5:22).

If there is a just cause for anger, we should not take the situation personally and we should not direct that anger against an individual to hurt him or her. Instead, we should use the emotional force as a motivation to correct the wrong if possible. Then, we should forgive the other individual involved and pray until the situation no longer has power over us. Regardless of the circumstances, temperance or self-control is part of the fruit of the Spirit that we should display (Galatians 5:23).

Clamor is noisy shouting, outcry, uproar, or insistent demand. Some people constantly complain. They clamor to get their way. Some adults throw temper tantrums and act as stubborn as small children who fall on the floor, scream, and kick. People who keep the church in an uproar—constantly demanding attention, always presenting demands, or blocking the progress of the church—are guilty of clamor. Scripture condemns this attitude and behavior.

Evil speaking comes from an evil heart. Much of it stems from jealousy. Do we allow ourselves to speak evil of people? Do we cause trouble by our speech? (See chapter 6 for further discussion of talebearing and reviling.)

Malice is active ill will, a desire to hurt others. Malice takes pleasure in causing someone to suffer or in seeing someone suffer. It is usually the result of hatred, which is like the sin of murder in the eyes of God (I John 3:15). We should hate sin but not the sinner. We can rejoice when sin is defeated but never in the misfortunes and sufferings of other people, even if they are sinners. Love does not rejoice in iniquity but only in the truth (I Corinthians 13:6).

Envy and jealousy are closely associated with bitterness, wrath, malice, and strife. Envy is resentment or ill will because of the advantages, possessions, or accomplishments of someone else. Jealousy is a resentful suspicion or rivalry. These attitudes often involve spite or greed.

Envy and strife are capable of producing any and every kind of evil (James 3:16). Envy is a work of the flesh that prevents people from going to Heaven (Galatians 5:21; James 4:5). This spirit surfaces unexpectedly in places where it should not be. People may get upset when someone else is used more in the church, is recognized more than they, receives certain favors, or even receives spiritual blessings.

Forgiveness

In place of all evil attitudes, Scripture exhorts us to be kind to one another, tenderhearted, and forgiving. Forgiveness is based on love and involves bearing the cost of someone else's mistake. It means giving up our rights in certain situations and ignoring certain things even when we know we are correct. It means swallowing our pride and asking others to forgive us even when we think they should be asking our pardon instead. It means turning the other cheek (Matthew 5:39).

Most importantly, forgiveness includes a decision to forget. Some people say, "I'll forgive, but I won't forget." They need to pray until they *can* forget; that is, until they no longer hold anything against someone. Some people pretend to forget but bring up an old grudge at a future confrontation. Or they may bring up an old mistake in order to gain some advantage over someone. This is not true forgiveness.

Forgiveness does not mean saying someone is right when they have done evil or saying their actions do not matter. Nor does it mean making ourselves vulnerable to those who have harmed us, thereby enabling them to harm us again. But it does mean refusing to retaliate with evil and refusing to harbor bitterness. It means putting the past behind us and being willing to accept sincere repentance.

Jesus plainly taught that God will forgive us only as much as we forgive others (Matthew 6:12, 14-15; 18:23-35). If we want to be forgiven of our sins, we must learn to forgive our brothers and sisters when they make mistakes.

A Root of Bitterness

Some people seemingly can never be satisfied. They murmur, complain, refuse to cooperate, and are self-willed. They cannot accept correction without becoming angry. They are busybodies, they sow discord in the church, they are talebearers, and they cause problems everywhere they go. What is wrong? It could be that they have a root of bitterness. "Looking diligently lest any man fail of the grace of God; lest any root of bitterness springing up trouble you, and thereby many be defiled" (Hebrews 12:15).

Significantly, this statement comes immediately after the admonition to follow peace and holiness (verse 14). In other words, bitterness will defile our holiness. The implication is that having a proper attitude is the most important aspect of holiness.

A root of bitterness is a source of bitterness. It is something in the heart that causes the outward manifestations we have identified. From this root many types of fruit come forth, none of which is the fruit of the Spirit. The actual root could be a grudge, jealousy, a wrong done to us that we have not turned over to God, or something else in our heart that we have never surrendered to God. If we develop a bad attitude, we should check for a source of bitterness in our heart. We must cut it out and destroy it so that we can bear enjoyable fruit.

We do not have the authority to judge the motives or heart of others, but we can observe fruit. If we see an apple growing on a tree, we know that it is an apple tree. The fruit speaks for itself. Likewise, when someone has a root of bitterness, the fruit will be easy to observe. Without attempting to judge the person, we can know enough to avoid participating in the gossip, envy, hatred, and strife that come out of that source. We can refuse to partake of such fruit, lest we be one of the many who are defiled by that person's root of bitterness.

Nothing Shall Offend

The Christian's attitude stands in stark contrast to the root of bitterness and all of its resulting attitudes. "Great peace have they which love thy law: and nothing shall offend them" (Psalm 119:165). Peace is the result of loving God and His Word (Philippians 4:7). Peace is one of the results of being justified (counted as righteous in the sight of God) (Romans 5:1).

An offense is something that causes a person to stumble in his or her walk with God. God's Word teaches us not to let anything offend us (cause us to stumble) and not to offend others (cause others to stumble). (See Matthew 5:29-30; 13:41; James 3:2.) Nothing will be a stumbling block to those who love the Word of God.

We sometimes hear complaints such as the following: "They invited others, but they did not invite me." "They asked others to do something at church but not me." "They never ask me to participate." "I was entitled to a certain thing because of my position or age, but they did not give it to me." "They did not speak to me." How many times have our feelings been hurt because we were rebuked, misunderstood, or overlooked? In all these cases, let us remember: "Nothing shall offend." Perhaps there were good reasons for a certain action that we do not know about, perhaps we did not get the true story, or perhaps someone made a mistake.

Regardless of the circumstances, we cannot allow ourselves to develop a bad attitude or lose our faith in God and in the church. We need an attitude of forgiveness when it appears that others have mistreated us—even if they do not ask forgiveness. When we pray the Lord's Prayer, we ask God to forgive us as much as we forgive others! (See Matthew 6:12-15.) Even when there is a violation of custom or etiquette, and even if we are in the right, we cannot allow ourselves to develop a bitter, unforgiving spirit. If we love God, then we will not let anything become a stumbling block to us. No matter what happens, we will not stumble and fall.

It may seem humanly impossible to respond positively to negative situations, but God gives us the power to overcome. Instead of complaining, "I am offended," or "Someone hurt my feelings," let us pray until God gives us victory in every situation.

Attitude When Corrected

We must maintain this determination in times of rebuke or reproof. "Shew me thy ways, O LORD; teach me thy paths" (Psalm 25:4). Some people think they never need instruction, correction, rebuke, reproof, or exhortation. But the Word of God says we do. God has placed government in the church, and everyone from the highest in position to the lowest is subject to godly authority. Even Peter and Paul accepted rebuke from others (Galatians 2:11-14; Acts 23:3-5). People who do not wish to submit to spiritual authority are on their way to apostasy (II Peter 2:10).

Let us never esteem ourselves so highly that we cannot accept admonition, rebuke, or exhortation. When someone in spiritual authority admonishes us out of love and faithfulness, we should carefully consider the admonition with the attitude of "Thank you for trying to help me"—not "I'm just as spiritual as you are, and you have made mistakes too, so I don't need to listen to you."

Hebrews 13:17 says, "Obey them that have the rule over you, and submit yourselves: for they watch for your souls, as they that must give account, that they may do it with joy, and not with grief: for that is unprofitable for you." This admonition applies to all believers, including leaders, and it teaches some important principles. First, God has ordained leaders in the church. He has organized a system of church government.

Second, we are to be humble and obedient. "To obey is better than sacrifice. . . . For rebellion is as the sin of witchcraft" (I Samuel 15:22-23). Third, true leaders have a duty to watch over our souls. If they see something sinful or dangerous, they have an obligation to warn us. We should accept their warning without becoming angry, for they are merely fulfilling their duty. Fourth, leaders are responsible to God. Whether they warn us or not is between them and God. Whether we listen and submit is between us and God. Finally, God will be our judge, and all rebellion against His authority will be unprofitable for us.

If we are wise, we will accept reproof (Proverbs 17:10). Just a few words of admonition are sufficient if we have the proper attitude. If we think we are beyond reproof, then we place ourselves in the position of a scoffer or a wicked person. If we are wise, we will love the godly leader or friend who rebukes us. (See Proverbs 9:7-9.) Both those giving a rebuke and receiving a rebuke must have the proper attitude in order for there to be good results.

Can a leader be rebuked? Nothing in Scripture suggests that a minister or other leader is exempt from these guidelines. Of course, the rebuke must come from someone with the proper spiritual authority. Even elders (pastors) who live in sin should be rebuked before others, so that everyone may learn (I Timothy 5:20). Unfortunately, when some are rebuked they receive so much sympathy and comfort from "friends" that they do not repent but instead become rebellious. In this case, no one learns what God intended.

Preachers are authorized, and indeed commanded, to use the Word to reprove (correct or convince), rebuke, and exhort (encourage) (II Timothy 3:16; 4:2). Consequently, let us always have the proper attitude when we receive admonition. Let us pray, "Show me your ways, Lord. Lead me. When I stray, send someone or something to correct me before it is too late. Help me to have a good attitude when I listen to messages or even to personal admonition. Help me not to make excuses, justify myself, or rebel against godly authority, but teach me to obey. Give me leaders who love me enough to teach me the truth and correct me when I need it."

Murmuring and Complaining

According to Jude 15-16, those who murmur (grumble) and complain (find fault) are ungodly. When differences arise, Christians are to pray for one another and encourage one another, not attack one another (Philippians 2:14). If there is a problem between two people, they should seek reconciliation without spreading the problem to others, and if necessary they can go to church leaders (Matthew 18:15-18). Instead, if they complain and murmur by talking or writing, they can become guilty of sowing discord.

It does not take much to tempt the average person or congregation to complain. Small inconveniences or the temporary lack of water, food, clothing, or money will test everyone. If we do not allow God to guide us, we easily become prisoners of our desires, appetites, and passions.

The Israelites, for example, began to complain about everything in the second month of their journey through the wilderness (Exodus 16:1-3). In Exodus alone we find twelve major complaints of Israel against God's plan and God's chosen leader. Their complaining stemmed from unbelief and a lack of respect for God's appointed leadership. Because of their unbelief they ended up traveling for forty years on a journey that should have taken only a few months.

Jude 11 teaches us to avoid the rebellion of Korah. This man criticized Moses and challenged his spiritual authority. Consequently, God caused the earth to swallow him and his followers. When Miriam and Aaron criticized Moses, the Lord heard it (Numbers 12:2). Although Miriam and Aaron were the older siblings of Moses, God rebuked them just the same. "Were ye not afraid to speak against my servant?" God asked (Numbers 12:8). Miriam was stricken with leprosy for seven days as punishment for her sin.

Paul learned "in whatsoever state I am, therewith to be content" (Philippians 4:11). When we feel mistreated, the solution is not to murmur and complain. Rather, we will find our answer through prayer. If applicable and necessary, we should talk directly to the person who has created the unpleasant situation. But we should not seek to avenge ourselves, for that prerogative belongs to God alone (Romans 12:19).

We find an excellent example of the proper attitude in David's relationship to Saul. Saul clearly wronged David, even trying to take his life. Saul had sinned to the point where God rejected him, and Samuel had already anointed David to be the next king. Yet, on two occasions, David refused to kill Saul when he had the chance to do so. As long as Saul was king, David did not want to harm him. David waited for God to remove Saul.

Instead of grumbling and finding fault, let us learn to be content, to pray, and to talk about situations to the right people with the right attitude. There is no use in confronting a matter if we cannot speak with a humble, quiet, forgiving spirit.

Complaining is contagious. It is also contrary to the Word of the Lord.

Proper Relationships with Fellow Believers

In addition to having a proper relationship with leaders, we need a proper relationship with fellow believers. Busybodies are inquisitive about other people's personal affairs, meddlers in the business of others, people who are busy with matters that should not concern them. I Peter 4:15 tells us not to suffer "as a busybody in other men's matters." Paul also warned against busybodies (II Thessalonians 3:11; I Timothy 5:13). According to Proverbs 20:3, a meddler is a fool.

Busybodies seem to know a little about everyone else's business and involve themselves in all kinds of problems. Often they try to interfere with the disciplining of an individual and try to "solve problems" without working with the pastor. Most of the time they do not help, but they just add more wood to the fire. Such people are a curse to a neighborhood and a plague to a church. These people try to find out everything that is going on. They feel that they are important and that they know everything. Actually they cannot be trusted with any important job that requires keeping things in confidence. As a result, a busybody does not qualify for the ministry.

We should examine ourselves to see if we have the tendency to be a busybody. If we are inquisitive by nature, we must let the Holy Spirit deliver us from excessive curiosity concerning other people's lives. In respecting others' lives we maintain proper relationships with our brothers and sisters.

Humility

The Bible maks it clear that a humble spirit is a prerequisite for healthy Christian living. God hates a proud look (Proverbs 6:17). He resists the proud but gives grace to the humble (James 4:6). Pride was the sin that caused Satan to fall, and it will cause the downfall and destruction of all who harbor it (Isaiah 14:12-15; Proverbs 16:18). The pride of life is one of the three basic categories of worldliness that tempt Christians (I John 2:16). John the Baptist and Jesus preached their harshest sermons against the hypocrisy and pride of religious people. Remarkably, they did not direct these vehement statements at the acknowledged sinners but at the spiritual leaders of their day. Clearly, religious people are susceptible to the sin of pride.

When talking about holiness, it is easy to become self-righteous and critical of others. It is possible to look holy but to be full of pride and hypocrisy, and in such a case we will not be justified in the sight of God. As an example, God rejected the pious prayer of a self-righteous Pharisee but heard the sincere cry of repentance from a sinful tax collector (Luke 18:9-14).

We must not let pride enter our hearts because we know truth and follow after holiness. Nor can we allow ourselves to develop the appearance of pride.

Preachers are susceptible in both areas. Since God hates a proud look, we should be careful how we conduct ourselves. Do we manifest pride in the way we speak to believers, in the way we sit on the platform, or even in the way we walk around with our Bibles?

No matter how spiritually mature we may be, we must always guard against pride. The more successful we are spiritually, the more the devil would like to tempt us with pride. We must seek after humility.

Even in this pursuit we must be careful, for some people try so hard to display humility that they actually appear to take pride in their so-called humility. True humility neither exalts nor disparages self but is not preoccupied with self. If we think we are very humble, then most likely we are not. If we rejoice in the attainment of great humility, then probably we have just lost it.

We can eradicate pride through prayer—the kind of prayer in which we fall down on our faces before God, lie prostrate before Him, and weep in His presence. We examine our hearts, and we ask God to reveal to us our true motives and attitudes. As we confess our faults, failures, inadequacies, and sins, we recognize the depth of our unworthiness and the magnitude of God's mercy and grace. This kind of prayer is not counted in minutes but in hours. After our spirit is broken and pride is washed away, then we can receive precious blessings and anointing from God. Such an experience is not something to boast of to others but to hide in our hearts. By periodically renewing this type of experience, we can guard against pride.

The Most Important Aspect of Holiness

In conclusion, a proper attitude is the most important aspect of holiness. A person with a humble, teachable attitude and a genuine desire to live for God can always be led to greater truth. Inward holiness will lead to outward holiness, but the reverse is not true. We often forget this, because it is easy to observe and compare outward holiness but more difficult to discern inward holiness. Outward holiness is often the easiest part to obey, while attitudes and spirits are more difficult to control.

A wrong attitude can be just as sinful as an act that we commit. Let us check our hearts for pride, murmuring, sowing discord, bitterness, wrath, and other evil attitudes. It would be sad to live in outward conformity to scriptural teachings yet destroy our life of holiness through an evil attitude that we allow to creep into our heart.

Session 3

Discussion Questions

1. What is the purpose of holiness in our lives?

2. Many times holiness is reduced only to outward standards, yet this session focuses on attitudes and inward principles. Why do you think these concepts are important concerning holiness?

3. Identify a fruit of the Spirit you strive to portray in your life and describe its connection to your pursuit of holiness.

4. Identify an attitude in which you need to improve in order to exemplify holy living, and explain how you intend to grow in this area.

Session 4

The Tongue: An Unruly Member

"But the tongue can no man tame; it is an unruly evil, full of deadly poison" (James 3:8).

"Let the words of my mouth . . . be acceptable in thy sight, O LORD" (Psalm 19:14).

The tongue is the most difficult member of the body to control, and it has the potential for causing the most harm. The way we use the tongue is a good indication of our relationship with God. The tongue speaks whatever is in the heart. If we speak evil, then evil must be in our heart, "for out of the abundance of the heart the mouth speaketh" (Matthew 12:34).

James contains strong teaching concerning the tongue. "If any man among you seem to be religious, and bridleth not his tongue, but deceiveth his own heart, this man's religion is vain" (James 1:26). "If any man offend not in word, the same is a perfect man, and able also to bridle the whole body" (James 3:2). The tongue is like a bit in a horse's mouth that controls the movements of the horse, a small helm that controls a large ship, and a small fire that can cause great trouble. The tongue can defile the whole body. Only the power of God can tame it (James 3:1-13).

The power of the tongue is apparently one reason why God has chosen speaking in tongues as the initial evidence of the Spirit baptism (Acts 2:4; 10:46; 19:6). We receive the Holy Spirit when we repent, believe, and surrender completely to God. Our tongue is the hardest member to tame, so it is the last part of us to yield to God. When we speak in tongues for the first time under the inspiration of the Spirit, it signifies that God has at last come inside and taken complete control.

James makes it clear that it is easy for us to sin with the tongue, that the tongue is dangerous, and that sinning with the tongue can destroy our holiness. Let us discuss some ways in which people sin with the tongue. Let us keep in mind that if it is wrong to speak some things, then it is wrong to listen to some things. Therefore, as we guard our tongue from evil, we should also guard our ear from evil, such as indulging in conversations or radio programs that are contrary to Christian values.

Talebearing or Gossip

Talebearing is a vicious sin. It is Satan's primary tool for destroying the church from within. It can destroy confidence in people, harm the innocent, and hinder the repentant. It splits churches, discourages saints, and disillusions new converts. The Bible teaches us to speak evil of no one, especially our brothers and sisters in the Lord (Titus 3:2; James 4:11; Psalm 101:5).

Most people will readily acknowledge the evils of talebearing, but the problem comes in identifying it in their own lives. It means telling things of a personal, intimate, or sensational nature that are harmful to someone. It involves damaging rumors and backbiting. Talebearing includes lying about someone or spreading negative rumors about someone, but it also includes telling facts of a personal, hurtful nature that the gossiper has no business revealing. Telling a fact can be

The Tongue: An Unruly Member

talebearing when it is told as gossip to someone who does not need to know about it.

God has ordained organization and authority in the church (I Corinthians 12:28). When problems arise in the church, those in authority should be informed. Leaders can and must judge situations in order to protect the flock (Matthew 18:18; I Corinthians 6:5).

However, needless disclosure to other members of the congregation is not right. Individuals are not to judge one another (Romans 14:10, 13; Matthew 7:1; James 4:12). Sometimes, information must be shared for clarification, instruction, or accuracy. In general, however, telling stories that could be harmful to others is not right in the sight of God (Proverbs 26:20, 22). How many churches would have peace if their members really believed the teachings of Scripture!

As a practical example, what should we do if we discover that a certain man in the church has committed adultery? We should not conceal the sin, for we do not have that authority. We should report the problem to someone in authority, such as the pastor, presbyter, or superintendent, depending on the person involved. At that point, the matter becomes the leader's responsibility. The reason is so the leader can help the sinning brother and also protect others in the church who may be affected by the sin. If we cover up the sin, we could cause great damage to individuals, families, and the whole body.

There is no reason to tell others about the sin, however. If we tell everyone else in the church we become a talebearer. If the brother has repented, why tell others about the sin? How will it help him if we tell everyone else of his fall? The problem is a private matter to be handled by the person, those in authority over him, and the Lord (Proverbs 11:13; 17:9).

As another example, suppose a person falls into sin, repents, and moves to another church. The former pastor should inform the new pastor so the latter may help the person, but it is generally not appropriate or necessary to tell the other church members about the problem.

We do not have the authority to cover up unrepented sin, regardless of whether a friend is involved or not. Nor should we cover up sin that would scripturally disqualify a person from holding a position. In both cases, the person in authority needs to know. At the same time, we do not need to tell a friend's sin to others.

A private sin becomes a church problem when the person does not repent but lives as a hypocrite or when the person brings disgrace and reproach upon the church. This point is especially relevant when someone in a position of leadership has sinned. For example, what if a deacon in the church commits adultery but repents? The pastor should be informed because it is a matter that could disgrace the whole church and because the deacon has lost the necessary qualifications, namely, a good report. The one with whom the deacon has sinned as well as anyone else who finds out about the sin will lose confidence in the church if nothing is done. This does not mean that the pastor should make a public announcement of the repented sin. The pastor can relieve the person of spiritual responsibilities without any explanation except that it was by mutual agreement.

In other situations, the pastor may put people on probation or silence them for a period of time. Of course, people should not speculate or gossip about what has happened. It may be best for wrongdoers simply to explain that they need to take some time for personal refreshing, renewing, and refocusing. Sometimes this is beneficial even when no sin has been committed, so the congregation should expect such occurrences without undue suspicion.

What should we do if we hear that someone has said or done something against us? First, since love thinks no evil, we should not be quick to believe the rumor. Instead, we should give the person the benefit of doubt and assume that the story is erroneous or that there is a good explanation. Then we should forget about the report.

Second, if the report still bothers us, we should pray for the Lord to give us peace. If the matter cannot be dismissed easily, then we should pray for the Lord to resolve the problem.

Third, if the problem persists even after prayer, we should go to the person who is involved, get the story straight from him or her, and clear up the problem (Matthew 18:15).

What should we do if we hear about serious wrongdoing on the part of someone else? We should take the first two steps just mentioned of not being quick to believe the rumor and praying about the situation. If the situation cannot be ignored, then we should report the matter to those in authority—typically, the pastor.

It then becomes the pastor's responsibility to deal with the situation. The pastor can speak to the individual as needed. If the pastor is convinced that the rumor is false, then he or she should advise those who heard it. If there is significant reason to believe that the story is true, then the pastor has a duty to deal with the situation. Either way, we should not pass along the story to other people.

If those in authority hear about a serious problem, they should go to the person who is allegedly involved and seek to clear up the matter. If leaders ask us to explain a matter involving us, we should not become offended, because they are simply fulfilling their responsibility. They are giving us an opportunity to clear up a misunderstanding, and we need to keep a good spirit in this situation. There is no need to find out who started the rumor or who told the leaders, because this could easily lead to vengeance and malice. It is the leaders' job to clear up the matter and, in the case of a false report, to rebuke or correct those who perpetuated the story. If we are indeed innocent, we should appreciate it when someone reports the situation to the pastor instead of repeating it to others.

Sowing Discord

The subject of talebearing is important because it is a principal means of sowing discord among believers. Sowing discord is one of seven abominations in Proverbs 6:16-19. An abomination is something God hates, and those who commit abominations will not go to Heaven (Revelation 21:8).

To sow discord means to cause dislike, distrust, and division, and it often occurs by talebearing or constant criticism. Those who sow discord think they can tell anything anywhere, anytime, to anyone. They repeat information they heard in confidence and obtained through friendship. They are not afraid to criticize anyone.

We need to examine ourselves in this area. Do we enjoy gossiping about people? Do we spread negative or injurious information about others instead of talking to them directly about our concerns? Do we enjoy hearing something bad about someone? Do we enjoy telling everything we know? Do we enjoy criticizing or laying blame on others? Do we stir up trouble, dissension, and strife? If any of these things is true, we need to change our ways. It does not matter how well we can preach or sing, if we sow discord we are in trouble with God.

Swearing

The term swearing has multiple meanings and is specifically mentioned in Scripture: "But above all things, my brethren, swear not, neither by heaven, neither by the earth, neither by any other oath . . . lest ye fall into condemnation" (James 5:12). Jesus said, "Swear not at all" (Matthew 5:34).

In the context of this lesson "swearing" means to assert something as true or promise something while under oath. An oath is a formal calling of God as a witness. The Bible teaches that we should not swear to anything or bind ourselves by an oath to do a certain thing or to join a certain group. Jesus explained that the law of Moses allowed people to swear by the Lord, but He instructed that under the new covenant we should not swear by anything—not by Heaven (i.e., God), earth, or even by our own heads. The reason is that we do not have the power to change any of these things, to enforce our oaths, or to guarantee our promises. (See Matthew 5:33-37.) God can swear by Himself because He has the power to make whatever He says come to pass. If something did not exist before, it becomes true the minute He speaks it.

When we are called upon by law to swear to something, we can simply say, "I affirm." To affirm means to state positively, to confirm, or to assert as valid. As human beings we do not have the power to swear by oath, but we can affirm that what we are saying is true. As Christians our word should always be true, and our promise should be just as good as any oath. We should have only one standard of truth. We do not need to use the words "I swear" to prove that at least we are telling the truth this one time, for people should always be able to depend on our word. We do not swear because we cannot control the things we would swear upon, but we can make sure that we always tell the truth and that we perform our promises to the best of our ability.

Taking God's Name in Vain

The commandments applicable today can be grouped into two categories: loving God and loving our neighbor (Mark 12:28-31). The commandment in Exodus 20:7 pertains to loving God by teaching us the proper use of His name: "Thou shalt not take the name of the Lord thy God in vain." It prohibits all profane, meaningless, trivial, or irreverent use of God's name. It also covers any abuse of His name in false oaths, false religions, and witchcraft. The right way to use

God's name is in praise, worship, preaching, teaching, prayer, and meditation.

The Jews were so careful about taking the name of the Lord in vain that they developed the custom of never pronouncing the name Jehovah or Yahweh. When reading aloud from the Hebrew Scriptures they would substitute the word *Adonai*, meaning Lord, for the sacred name Yahweh. When quoting or writing their Scriptures in Greek, they would use the Greek word *kurios*, which also means Lord. The writers of the New Testament followed this practice and so did the King James translators. For example, Isaiah 40:3 uses the Hebrew word Yahweh, which the translators represented by "LORD" (large and small capital letters). When Matthew quoted this verse in Greek, he used *kurios* (Matthew 3:3).

Unfortunately, many Christians treat God's name and titles casually. Often they will use the words *God, Lord, Jesus,* or *hallelujah* (which means "praise the Lord" in Hebrew) in a useless or lighthearted way. For many, it becomes a habit to use one of these words as a mere byword when they are happy, angry, sad, disappointed, or surprised. But we should only use these words when we are sincerely invoking God's help, communicating with Him, or talking about Him. If we use these words casually and thoughtlessly, then we diminish their value to inspire faith when we invoke them in prayer and praise. When we reserve these words for sincere, meaningful communication, then we show proper respect for God and preserve their value to inspire faith in the hearts of both speakers and hearers.

Slang

We should also be cautious when using slang expressions. Many slang words have negative connotations, and we can easily pick up a slang expression without realizing what it really means. What about watered down versions of curse words? If we do not want to use certain words, why use their derivatives and substitutes?

Filthy Communication

The Scripture establishes guidelines for a Christian's communication: "Put off . . . filthy communication out of your mouth" (Colossians 3:8). "Let no corrupt communication proceed out of your mouth" (Ephesians 4:29). We are the temple of the Holy Spirit, and as such we must not allow dirty jokes, words, and actions to come from us. Words that suggest something indecent should not come from the lips of a Christian. Should praises and vile words come out of the same mouth? "Doth a fountain send forth at the same place sweet water and bitter? Can the fig tree, my brethren, bear olive berries? either a vine, figs? so can no fountain both yield salt water and fresh" (James 3:11-12).

We are to have "neither filthiness, nor foolish talking, nor jesting" (Ephesians 5:4). This passage does not forbid entertainment, joking, or humor, but it tells us that holiness guidelines apply even in these activities. "Foolish talking" means idle, stupid talk. Jesting refers to coarse, obscene talk. In other words, Christians should not take part in smutty, insinuating, sexually oriented stories, jokes, or actions. It is a shame even to talk about some things that are done in secret (Ephesians 5:12). Some things may be appropriate to discuss in a proper setting but not in public or in mixed company. Some things should be kept in confidence between husband and wife. To do less is to profane the sacredness of marital intimacy.

Cursing

Another Christian principle for communication is to refrain from cursing: "Bless them which persecute you: bless, and curse not" (Romans 12:14). "Out of the same mouth proceedeth blessing and cursing. My brethren, these things ought not so to be" (James 3:10). These verses deal with the practice of pronouncing a curse upon someone. The Christian attitude is not to return evil for evil but to overcome evil with good (Romans 12:21). Jesus commanded, "Love your enemies, bless them that curse you, do good to them that hate you, and pray for them which despitefully use you, and persecute you" (Matthew 5:44).

Some ministers misunderstand their authority and abuse their position by pronouncing curses upon people. In one case, a woman and her family did something the pastor did not like. In retaliation, he verbally pronounced a curse upon her. As we have just seen, this practice is contrary to the Word of God. All genuine exercise of spiritual gifts must take place with love and for edification. (See I Corinthians 13:1-3; 14:3.)

Sometimes, people cite biblical examples to justify cursing. Let us examine the three primary examples they use: II Kings 2:23-24; Acts 5:3-10; and Acts 13:10-11.

In II Kings 2, a group of young men from the city of Bethel mocked the prophet Elisha. They called him a "bald head," an epithet of contempt and derision in the Old Testament that meant "worthless fellow." They taunted him, "Go up," that is, "Be translated as you say your master, Elijah, was." Elisha rebuked them in the name of the Lord. Later two bears came out and tore forty-two of them.

This incident occurred under the old covenant, not in the context of New Testament ministry. We should also note that these men were already under divine condemnation. They were from Bethel, one of the two cities in the northern kingdom of Israel that had erected golden calves to worship

(I Kings 12:29), and they were mocking the prophet of God and the power of God. Under the law, these men were already condemned to die because of their idolatry (Deuteronomy 13:12-15). God had already cursed them, and the question was simply when the judgment would be carried out. Because God does not always execute judgment speedily, people are prone to think that God has overlooked their sin (Ecclesiastes 8:11). In this case, God delayed His judgment until they began mocking His prophet. Elisha did not place them under a curse but pronounced that the time of God's judgment had come.

Acts 5 relates the story of Ananias and Sapphira. This couple tried to deceive the church by making a covenant to lie. God gave Peter a word of knowledge and revealed the truth to him. Peter did not personally curse Ananias and Sapphira but simply told Ananias that he was lying, whereupon God struck him dead. A short time later, God gave Peter another word of knowledge, and he prophesied that Sapphira would die just as her husband had.

When the law was first given, Aaron's disobedient sons suffered the penalty of death as an example to everyone of the importance of keeping God's Word (Leviticus 10:1-2). Similarly, Ananias and Sapphira died for their hypocrisy at the beginning of the New Testament church. Although hypocrites in the church do not generally die immediately, this example serves as a warning under the new covenant. In neither case did humans curse the offenders, however.

The last case concerns Paul and the sorcerer Barjesus, who opposed the preaching of the gospel in Cyprus. In this case, God gave Paul a word of knowledge as to what He was going to do, and Paul revealed it to Barjesus through prophecy. Paul said, "The hand of the Lord is upon thee, and thou shalt be blind" (Acts 13:11). Paul did not exhibit hatred or revenge, but this incident confirmed the truth of his message.

These examples do not give us the authority to curse other people, but they demonstrate the judgment of God upon sin. To curse someone would be in direct opposition to the Word of God. When people do something wrong, our attitude should be one of mercy and forgiveness. We should pray in love, "God, have mercy on them. Help them to understand their mistake, and lead them to repentance."

Reviling

To revile or to rail means to abuse using words; to use harsh, insolent, or abusive language. Since we are the temple of the Holy Spirit, we should not follow fleshly emotions but respond according to the Spirit. Even if we have been mistreated or misjudged, we should not revile other people (I Corinthians 6:10; 5:11). In I Corinthians 4:12-13 we find the proper reaction when others revile us. The apostles were reviled, persecuted, defamed, and made as the filth of the world. Their response was to bless.

Paul was rebuked for reviling the high priest while under questioning by the Sanhedrin council (Acts 23:1-5). Ananias, the priest, had commanded someone to slap Paul, which was contrary to the law. At the same time he was trying to judge Paul by the law. Paul quickly told Ananias that he was a "whited wall," or hypocrite, for doing this. When Paul said that, those standing by rebuked him for reviling God's high priest. When Paul realized that Ananias was the high priest, he apologized. He quoted Exodus 22:28, which prohibits the reviling of a ruler, and explained that he did not know he was speaking to the high priest when he said what he did. Either Paul did not know to whom he was speaking or he did not acknowledge the man's usurpation of office. In fact, according to history, Ananias usurped this office from which he had previously been expelled by the Romans for crimes. Paul recognized that even though he was being unjustly condemned, he should not revile the high priest, because of his office.

Even Michael the archangel did not bring a railing or reviling accusation against the devil when contending with him but simply said, "The Lord rebuke thee" (Jude 9). Michael did not abuse even Satan with words, remembering no doubt that Satan originally had been created as an anointed cherub. Jude contrasted Michael's good attitude with that of apostates who despise authority, speak evil of dignitaries, and speak evil of things they do not know (verses 8, 10).

Peter similarly described apostates, those who have forsaken truth to the point that they do not fear the Word of God. "But chiefly them that walk after the flesh in the lust of uncleanness, and despise government. Presumptuous are they, self-willed, they are not afraid to speak evil of dignities. Whereas angels, which are greater in power and might, bring not railing accusation against them before the Lord" (II Peter 2:10-11). These people do not want anyone to tell them what to do. They will not accept correction. They are not afraid to speak evil about those in authority over them. The fear of the Lord is the beginning of wisdom (Proverbs 9:10), but they have no fear or reverence for the Lord, His Word, His church, or His appointed leaders.

According to Peter and Jude, these people need to learn from the angels. The angels who have the responsibility to report to God about these same apostates do not rashly accuse or bitterly condemn them. They merely report the facts as they are without reviling or railing. They are courteous in their reports, even though they have more power than human beings.

Thus, we find that the apostles, including Paul, and the angels, including Michael, knew better than to revile. Yet many people do not hesitate to speak harshly to and about fellow believers, including leaders. Sometimes, believers speak disparagingly of their pastors, and ministers speak disparagingly about other ministers. Even if someone has sinned, however, there is a process by which to bring the matter before the proper authority. To report facts to those in authority is right, but to speak maliciously and to revile when reporting is wrong.

Jesus warned us to be careful of calling anyone a fool (Matthew 5:22). In the biblical context, this word connotes someone who is morally obstinate, not merely ignorant or simple. (See Psalm 14:1.) Thus, it represents strong condemnation and could become a means of reviling others.

Holiness teaches us not to speak evil about anyone and not to revile anyone. Even if people have sunk to the depths of sin, we should not revile them. We should be especially careful not to revile leaders. Those who revile are doing something that the apostles and the angels refused to do, even with regard to the worst sinners and the devil himself.

Lying and Bearing False Witness

"Thou shalt not bear false witness against thy neighbor" (Exodus 20:16; Mark 10:19). "All liars, shall have their part in the lake which burneth with fire and brimstone" (Revelation 21:8). Scripture shows us that God hates lies (Exodus 20:16; Mark 10:19; Revelation 21:8). Nothing that makes a lie, whether by speech or action, will enter into the New Jerusalem (Revelation 21:27). Two of the seven abominations (things God hates) in Proverbs 6:16-19 are a lying tongue and a false witness that speaks lies. Moreover, God wants us to keep our promises even if they hurt us (Psalm 15:4). In short, "he that speaketh lies shall not escape" (Proverbs 19:5).

To lie means to make a statement knowing that it is false or to say something with the intent to deceive. It can also involve deliberately giving a false impression to someone who has a right and expectation to know the full truth. In certain situations, it can even be dishonest to tell part of the truth—for example, if the effect is to conceal additional truth that is necessary to understand a situation correctly from someone

The Tongue: An Unruly Member

who has a right to know. For this reason, we are to tell the truth, the whole truth, and nothing but the truth in a court of law.

A lie is a lie even if told for a good purpose. The end does not justify the means. For instance, suppose two people have an argument and refuse to speak to each other. A third person decides to be a mediator and falsely tells each person that the other has already apologized. Even though the purpose is to bring reconciliation, the third person has told a lie.

Suppose a teenager has parents who will not let him attend church. Should he lie about where he is going in order to attend? No, he should not commit sin in order to go to church. Suppose a woman is married to an unbelieving husband, and he forbids her to pay tithes on his income. She promises not to do so, but should she secretly give this money to the church anyway? No, she has given her word, and she would be lying if she broke it. She would defraud her husband and destroy his confidence in her.

Some cite the story of Rahab to demonstrate that the end justifies the means, because she lied to the people of Jericho in order to conceal Israelite spies. However, she was a Gentile who did not know the law of God. She heard about the great things Jehovah had done for Israel, and she believed in Him. As a result, she hid the spies and assisted them in their mission. She was not saved by lying but by her faith as demonstrated by works. God wanted to show His power through Israel so that all nations would see it, believe on Him, and be saved. Rahab was one person who obeyed this plan. If she had known God's law and had prayed accordingly, God could have made another way to deliver the spies. Moreover, this example involves concealment in order to save human life, and thus it would not justify lying in lesser circumstances.

Abraham lied on two occasions by saying that his wife, Sarah, was only his sister (Genesis 12:10-20; 20:1-16). He did this because he feared that foreign kings would kill him in order to marry Sarah, who was very beautiful. Sarah actually was Abraham's half sister, but he was dishonest in not telling these potential suitors that she was also his wife. Both times his deception almost led to disaster, since the kings tried to take Sarah as their wife, thinking she was available. Only the intervention of God restored her to Abraham. Abraham was reproved for his deception both times and was even expelled from the land one time. These incidents show that lying is wrong even when the purpose is to protect our legitimate interests, that lying causes more problems than it solves, that God can deliver us from difficult situations without our resorting to lies, and that telling a half-truth in order to create a false impression can be a lie.

On the other hand, we are not necessarily obligated to disclose everything we know about a situation, especially to someone who does not have a right to know this private information. In order to protect Samuel from the potential wrath of King Saul when Samuel went to anoint David as the future king of Israel, God told him to go to Bethlehem to offer a sacrifice. If someone were to inquire about his trip, he could honestly say that he was offering a sacrifice; he would not need to volunteer that he was also on a secret mission to anoint David. (See I Samuel 16:1-5.)

It is possible to "make a lie" by actions as well as words. What if a minister displays a false graduation diploma as if he had earned it? He is lying by giving a false impression. What if an office worker submits a receipt for reimbursement but actually the expense was less than the receipt shows? She has lied and committed fraud. Similarly, what if a worker requisitions money for one thing but spends it on something else? He has lied, unless he obtains authorization for the change. What if he does not spend the full amount of the requisition but pockets the difference? He has lied and committed fraud.

As Christians we do not have to lie. If we have not done anything wrong, we can trust God to help us and protect us in difficult situations. From an eternal perspective the old saying is true: Honesty is the best policy.

Careless Words

Jesus said, "Out of the abundance of the heart the mouth speaketh. . . . Every idle word that men shall speak, they shall give account thereof in the day of judgment. For by thy words thou shalt be justified, and by thy words thou shalt be condemned" (Matthew 12:34, 36-37). If we speak carelessly, we could easily commit sin and could easily harm others. Therefore, we should think before we speak. What we talk about reveals what is in our heart, and what is in our heart determines whether we are living by faith in Jesus Christ.

Importance of the Tongue

These words of Jesus demonstrate how important our speech is. As we noted at the beginning of this chapter, James 1:26 warns, "If any man among you seem to be religious, and bridleth not his tongue, but deceiveth his own heart, this man's religion is vain." On the other hand, "if any man offend not in word, the same is a perfect man, and able also to bridle the whole body" (James 3:2). In short, we need to have "sound speech, that cannot be condemned" (Titus 2:8). "Let your speech be alway with grace, seasoned with salt, that ye may know how ye ought to answer every man" (Colossians 4:6).

Ultimately, only God can help us control our tongues, so we must pray for His guidance and grace in this matter. "Let the words of my mouth . . . be acceptable in thy sight, O Lord" (Psalm 19:14). "Set a watch, O Lord, before my mouth; keep the door of my lips" (Psalm 141:3).

7

The Eye: The Light of the Body

"The light of the body is the eye. . . . If thine eye be evil, thy whole body shall be full of darkness" (Matthew 6:22-23).

"I will set no wicked thing before mine eyes" (Psalm 101:3).

Gate of the Soul

David made a covenant with his eyes when he promised not to place any wicked thing in front of them. He also asked God to "turn away mine eyes from beholding vanity" (Psalm 119:37). Vanity refers to anything that is worthless, foolish, empty, and destitute of reality. Why did David place such emphasis on keeping his eyes free from beholding wicked and vain things?

The reason is that the eye is a unique member of the body in certain important respects. Jesus told us that the eye is the light of the body (Matthew 6:22-23; Luke 11:34). If it is "single" (clear, whole, not blinded), then the whole body will be full of light. If it is "evil" (wicked, diseased, blind), then the whole body will be full of darkness. If the light of the body is dark, how great is the darkness of the rest of the body! In other words, Jesus taught that the eye is the gate to the heart or soul. It is the principal sensory organ that we use to receive information from the outside world. If our eye is constantly filled with evil sights, then our thoughts and actions will be drastically affected.

Psychologists have verified this statement, estimating that 90 percent of our thought life is stimulated by what we see. Experiments have shown that the human brain retains in long-term memory about 65 percent of what it receives through the eyes and ears simultaneously but only about 15 percent of what comes through the ears alone. As a simple illustration of the impact of the eyes on the mind, we can think of the difference between seeing a horrible accident as opposed to merely hearing about it. There is much truth in the old saying, "Seeing is believing."

What we see has a powerful influence on our thoughts. In turn, our thoughts determine what kind of people we are. "For as he thinketh in his heart, so is he" (Proverbs 23:7). As Jesus said, the condition of the eyes determines the condition of the body as a whole. What the eyes indulge in and enjoy is what the body will indulge in and enjoy. For this reason, the "lust of the eyes" is one of the three major areas of worldliness and temptation (I John 2:16). While we can be tempted through other senses, the Bible does not speak of the lust of the nose or ears, because their influence is not nearly as significant as that of the eyes.

Temptation is the first step toward sin, and after lust has conceived it brings forth sin (James 1:14-15). Often, temptation comes through the eyes. Eve saw that the forbidden fruit was pleasant to the eye, so she took it (Genesis 3:6). Achan saw a garment, some silver, and some gold. God had forbidden the Israelites from taking anything from Jericho, and no doubt Achan intended to obey, but when he actually saw these objects he explained, "Then I coveted them" (Joshua 7:21). David "saw a woman washing herself; and the woman was very beautiful to look upon" (II Samuel 11:2). This temptation led directly to adultery and eventually murder. Satan showed Jesus the kingdoms of the world from a mountaintop in order to tempt Him (Matthew 4:8). All these incidents show how powerful the eyes can be.

Satan knows that he can easily reach the mind through the eye. He tries to bring temptations before our eyes for several reasons. First, in this way we encounter suggestions we had not previously known about or considered. Second, scenes can become embedded in our memories so that they are available to tempt us later when we are weak or discouraged. Third, constant exposure to certain sights and their associated ideas causes us gradually to become accustomed to them. We may eventually come to accept them as permissible, normal, or inevitable. Finally, if we think about certain things long enough, we will eventually sin—whether by entertaining and dwelling on these scenes in our minds or by committing an outward act of sin.

We must guard our eyes from temptations. Of course, many situations present themselves to us and yet we may have little control over them. For example, we may see immodest dress almost anywhere today. What should we as Christians do in this kind of situation? We may not be able to avoid such sights completely, but we can discipline our eyes and minds. We must not entertain, fantasize about, or deliberately prolong the temptation; for doing so can lead to sin, either in our minds or in our actions.

Scriptural Guidelines for Media

There are areas in modern society where we are able to exercise complete control over what we allow our eyes to see; namely, the use of visual media, including both printed and electronic materials. Let us look at some passages of Scripture that apply to our use of these media.

As we have discussed, evil can easily enter our minds through our eyes. Thus, whatever we are supposed to keep out of our minds, we should keep away from our eyes. Jesus said, "For out of the heart proceed evil thoughts, murders, adulteries, fornications, thefts, false witness, blasphemies: these are the things which defile a man" (Matthew 15:19-20). Isaiah 33:15-16 gives this promise: he "that stoppeth his ears from hearing of blood, and shutteth his eyes from seeing evil; he shall dwell on high."

Paul commanded, "Abstain from all appearance of evil" (I Thessalonians 5:22). After listing twenty-three sins of debased people, he further described them as follows: "who knowing the judgment of God, that they which commit such things are worthy of death, not only do the same, but have pleasure in them that do them" (Romans 1:32). Not only is it wrong to commit evil, but it is also wrong to take pleasure in others who commit evil. Thus, we should not entertain ourselves by the depiction and glorification of evil deeds. When we do, we think defiling thoughts. How can we take pleasure in the sins of others and yet fulfill the commandment, "Ye that love the LORD, hate evil" (Psalm 97:10)? As the psalmist prayed, "Let the words of my mouth, and the meditation of my heart, be acceptable in thy sight, O LORD" (Psalm 19:14).

Reading

Reading is one of the best means of self-education. Someone who loves to read will probably have a large vocabulary, good grammar, and a general knowledge of a variety of topics. Reading helps to keep the mind active. It can be a valuable source for intelligent conversation, preaching, and teaching. There are many good books and magazines, both fiction and nonfiction.

At the same time, some reading material is not suitable for Christians. Examples are novels that glorify immorality or violence, explicit and graphic descriptions of sex, books filled with obscene and blasphemous words, pornographic magazines, magazines that focus on intimate confessions and scandals, and books that deal with witchcraft and the occult. If we feed on this type of material, then we will not have clean hearts. We must put away such books from our lives and destroy those in our possession, as did the church in Ephesus (Acts 19:19). If we read certain descriptions and absorb certain scenes, we plant them in our heart, and eventually they will proceed out of the heart.

If in doubt about whether to read something or not, we can ask: Are these meditations acceptable in the sight of God? The Holy Spirit will guide us in specific situations. Let us be sensitive to the Spirit and to the impressions He gives. We also have the laws of God written upon our hearts by faith, so our conscience, as informed by Scripture, can be a helpful guide. When we begin to read something that is unwholesome, the Holy Spirit can impress us not to continue. If we continue, our conscience will bother us. At that point, we have power either to suppress the voice of conscience or to obey it and do God's will.

Some say that novels are frivolous and unwholesome, but the reading of fiction can be a valid form of recreation and refreshment. Moreover, good fiction can stimulate thought, impart information, and increase language skills. Some types of fiction, such as comic books, may have little or no informative or educational value. It is advisable to limit the reading of this type of material and for parents to monitor and control its use.

Viewing

Technology has created many forms of visual media, including television programing, movies and digital media delivered via the Internet, video games, CDs, DVDs, smart phones, and tablets. These media are a major area of concern in our day with respect to the lust of the eyes. As Christians, we should carefully regulate all use of media. While entertainment is not wrong, we must exercise great care when seeking entertainment in modern culture.

In making these decisions, we seek to implement the teachings of Psalm 101:2-3: "I will behave myself wisely in a perfect way. O when wilt thou come unto me? I will walk within my house with a perfect heart. I will set no wicked thing before mine eyes: I hate the work of them that turn aside; it shall not cleave to me." While we cannot prevent all temptations from coming to us, we should exercise control in areas of our own responsibility, especially the home. We also seek to follow Romans 1:32, which teaches that people who take pleasure in watching others commit sin are guilty of sin as well.

Technology is rapidly changing, leading to a proliferation of new choices and a merging with old choices. Thus, each generation needs to evaluate the situation in its day in order to make responsible Christian choices.

The scope of the problem becomes clear when we see the results of a 2012 report commissioned by the Dove Foundation. Covering the top 1,000 movies released from 2005-2009, this study shows that 38 percent were rated R; 41 percent, PG-13; 18 percent, PG; and only 3 percent were rated G.

With regard to other digital media such as DVDs and the Internet we recognize that there is greater ability to make and regulate choices, so that people can choose to watch things that are wholesome, beneficial, inspirational, or educational.

However, whatever is objectionable to watch on television or in movie theaters is objectionable to watch using these media. In all use of technology, we should only allow ourselves to view things that are consistent with family and Christian values. We also need to consider and follow the admonition of our pastor in this area. In all cases, parents should communicate clear guidelines to their children and personally monitor their viewing activities. Some good questions to ask are: Would I be comfortable showing this at church? Would I be willing to invite the pastor to watch with me?

For Internet use, we recommend placing the computer in a common area where its use can easily be seen by others and using a filtering program to block unwholesome sites. As a safeguard, parents should be able to monitor children's use, and a spouse should be able to monitor a spouse's use. It is wise for parents to instruct children to obtain their permission whenever they wish to use the Internet.

In selecting various visual media, we should carefully research their appropriateness for Christian viewing. Filtering guards can eliminate the occasional, unexpected use of inappropriate language. Detailed reviews are available online to assist in making wise decisions. Appropriate versions can also be purchased online from Christian or family-oriented companies.

For video games, we have instructed our children not to play anything that involves their killing of humans, that graphically depicts bloodshed, or that promotes immorality. We monitor both content and use of time. A rating of T (teen) indicates content that is potentially inappropriate, while M (mature) and A (adult) are clearly contrary to Christian values.

The problem with television, movies, and other media. The kinds of things displayed on the screen are generally not conducive to Christian living. Violence and sex are the two most common topics. Immodest clothing, assault, adultery, fornication, lying, hatred, cursing, drinking, smoking, filthy speech, and murder are among the evils shown almost constantly. This list sounds remarkably like the things in Matthew 15:19-20 that defile a person. Most of the programming consists of activities in which Christians should not participate. The scriptural admonitions, "I will set no wicked thing before mine eyes," "Abstain from all appearance of evil," and "Let the meditation of my heart be acceptable," are all applicable. How can we profess to hate evil if we indulge in watching these scenes? How can we avoid the condemnation of Romans 1:32 on those who take pleasure in watching others sin?

The viewer is bombarded with evil scenes and ungodly behavior. This evil goes directly from the eyes to the heart or mind. The result is to undermine resistance to sin. The mind is constantly tempted and encouraged to sin. By seeing sin repeated over and over, the mind becomes desensitized and gradually comes to the conclusion that it is not so bad after all. Viewers subconsciously assume that society in general is similar to what they see on the screen and that everyone else is living that way. The result is a compromising and permissive attitude.

As psychologists verify, television and movies are a form of escapism. The mind subconsciously identifies with the actors and plays their roles as a means of escaping the drudgery of life. Thus, the viewer's mind is polluted by participating vicariously in unwholesome scenes. In short, television and movies are a source of temptation and pollution of the heart or mind. They gradually erode defenses and alter attitudes toward sin through subtle influences. They entertain the carnal nature and feed the lusts of the flesh. Constant viewing of the standard fare of television and movies undermines spirituality.

Medical doctors, psychologists, sociologists, and social commentators have researched the effects of television on the human mind, especially on the mind of children. The following sources report some of these findings and describe the power and danger of television from a secular point of view. Although the comments are directed primarily toward television, they apply to other visual media when used in the same manner.

Michael and Diane Medved, authors of *Saving Childhood*, offer commentary on media in the home. The authors are a Jewish couple; he is a radio talk show host and former film critic, while she is a psychologist in private practice. They describe how modern culture destroys the innocence of childhood, leading to much of the dysfunctional and destructive behaviors in society today. In response, parents need to protect their children from these assaults and provide children with security, a sense of wonder, and optimism (faith).

According to the A.C. Nielsen Company, the average American watches more than twenty-eight hours of television a week. This is the equivalent of nine uninterrupted *years* of a sixty-five-year life. Some studies show that by age five a child will have spent more time watching TV than talking to his or her father in a *lifetime*. The Medveds conclude: "Our strongest suggestion for maintaining your kids' sense of wonder is *cut out—or cut down on—*TV. . . . The problem is not too much sex or too much sleaze or too much violence, *it's too much TV—period*." Their solution is as follows:

The Medved family has never owned a TV. . . . Upon proposing to Diane, Michael had one potentially deal-breaking stipulation: no TV. . . . We do own a video monitor, however, though absence of any antenna or cable makes TV reception impossible. We allow our three children to watch selected and approved videos that we own or rent, up to six hours a week.

Internet usage is even more prevalent with the Pew Research Center reporting that 81 percent of all American adults (eighteen years old and up) and 95 percent of all American teens use the Internet with social interaction taking up most of their time. A 2009 Harris poll reported that 14 percent of adult Internet users spent over twenty-four hours a week on the Internet while eight to eighteen year olds spend an average of 53 hours a week on the Internet. These statistics underscore the need to guard against excessive use of media and its potential to steer individuals and families away from other Christian priorities.

Summary

We have abundant evidence of the adverse spiritual, mental, emotional, and physical effects of unwholesome media programing. It feeds the lusts of the flesh, is a constant source of temptation, is a thief of time, harms family life, damages children's character and morals, promotes sin, and is psychologically detrimental. Under these circumstances, Christians are better off without its influence. As technology continues to change and new options and new circumstances develop, Christians should carefully regulate all use of visual media in accordance with Christian values.

What is the position of Christians who habitually watch worldly programming on television and other media? Do they still hate evil? Apparently, their love is in the wrong place. This position is dangerous, for "if any man love the world, the love of the Father is not in him" (I John 2:15). If we bring unwholesome programs into the home through television, the Internet, and other media, it will be difficult for us to mind the things of the Spirit and to maintain a close walk with God. Worldly programming will sap our power with God and subtly influence us in the wrong direction.

Since not all content is sinful, we cannot say that watching one program is necessarily a sin, but regular viewing can be detrimental or dangerous. Because much of the content is sinful, frequent viewing is likely to lead to sin, for it is difficult to avoid all inappropriate content when it is so readily available. It is sinful to indulge in carnal lusts and to take pleasure in evil.

We should note the importance of following personal convictions in this area. Whatever is not of faith is sin (Romans 14:23), and a knowing failure to do what is good is sin (James 4:17). We should also heed the words of the wise man in Ecclesiastes 7:29: "God hath made man upright; but they have sought out many inventions."

Session 4

Discussion Questions

1. Why do you think holiness in speech is important?

2. How could holiness in our speech be connected to the Christian attitudes we discussed in the last session?

3. Media consumption is certainly a relevant topic in our society. How do you set guardrails for what is acceptable on your media devices?

4. How do scriptural principles on what we should and shouldn't look at relate to your overall pursuit of holiness?

5. How do you evaluate acceptable media for your children?

Session 5

8

Scriptural Apparel and Adornment

"In like manner also, that women adorn themselves in modest apparel, with shamefacedness and sobriety; not with broided hair, or gold, or pearls, or costly array" (I Timothy 2:9).

"The woman shall not wear that which pertaineth unto a man, neither shall a man put on a woman's garment: for all that do so are abomination unto the LORD thy God" (Deuteronomy 22:5).

Outward appearance is an important aspect of holiness. The Bible teaches Christians how to dress and how to adorn themselves, giving principles that govern the outward appearance.

It is important to understand principles in this area for at least two reasons. First, styles of dress and customs have changed since the days of the Bible, so we must apply its teachings to situations unknown in that day. Second, few statements in the New Testament specifically deal with men's appearance, since men's adornment was generally not a problem in those days. By identifying principles, we can apply the teaching to both men and women. Thus, in this chapter we discuss five scriptural principles for adornment and dress.

Modesty

We begin by recognizing the fundamental principle that Christians are to be modest in their appearance (I Timothy 2:9). The Greek word for "modest" is *kosmios*, which means orderly, well-arranged, decent, modest. Here it describes someone who is decent or chaste, especially in outward dress and deportment. In explaining how women should adorn themselves, the apostle Peter explained that wives can win their unsaved husbands by their chaste conduct (I Peter 3:2). Modesty is particularly important when we appear in public in view of the opposite sex.

In the beginning, God created Adam and Eve in a state of innocence, and it seems that they were clothed with His glory. (See Genesis 2:25; Psalm 8:5.) Their relationship of physical, mental, and spiritual union was pure. When they sinned against God by eating fruit of the tree of knowledge of good and evil, they lost God's glory, realized they were naked, and tried to clothe themselves with fig leaves. The pure relationship between man and woman was now capable of being distorted and polluted by sin, especially as the human race multiplied. Thus, God clothed Adam and Eve with animal skins to cover their nakedness (Genesis 3:21). Since that time, it has been His plan for humans to be decently clothed.

The devil tries to do just the opposite to humans. One of the things the demon-possessed man of Gadara did was take off his clothes. When Jesus cast out the demons, the man was found fully clothed and in his right mind (Luke 8:27, 35).

Immodest apparel can indicate the presence of a lustful spirit—a desire to flaunt the body and to attract the opposite sex by lust. Immodesty is a strong temptation and enticement, especially for men, who are more visually oriented and more easily aroused than women. David fell into adultery because of the lust of the eyes (II Samuel 11:2). It is easy for a man to sin in his heart by looking at an immodestly clothed woman (Matthew 5:28). In such a case the man is guilty, but the woman is not completely innocent either. God's plan for us today is to dress modestly.

Modest apparel means clothing that does not indecently expose the body to the opposite sex, whether intentionally or carelessly. In this regard, we should be mindful of sleeve length, necklines, dress length, tight clothes, and thin clothes. Both men and women need to develop a personal sense of modesty, wearing clothing that is appropriate to the occasion—whether sitting or standing, remaining still or praising God joyfully. For example, to implement the principle of modesty under various circumstances, we recommend that sleeves cover the upper arm and that dresses cover the knee.

Avoiding Personal Ornamentation

The word *modest* also has the connotation of not being showy or flashy. A woman should adorn herself with "shamefacedness and sobriety" and not with personal ornaments such as elaborately arranged hair (particularly braiding jewelry into the hair), gold, pearls, or extremely costly garments (I Timothy 2:9). "Shamefacedness" means reverence, self-restraint, modesty, and bashfulness. "Sobriety" means discretion, temperance, and self-control.

In short, Christians are not to dress in a vain way. God hates pride (see chapter 5), and He does not approve of a pretentious or ostentatious display. Styles primarily designed to feed the ego are not appropriate. Women should not rely on outward adorning to establish their identity. "Whose adorning let it not be that outward adorning of plaiting the hair, and of wearing of gold, or of putting on of apparel; but let it be the hidden man of the heart, in that which is not corruptible, even the ornament of a meek and quiet spirit, which is in the sight of God of great price" (I Peter 3:3-4).

It is acceptable to "adorn" oneself with "modest apparel." There is nothing wrong with ornamental aspects of clothing—such as colors, patterns, buttons, bows, scarves, and ties—as long as they remain in moderation. Clothing should be primarily functional and only secondarily ornamental. However, Scripture specifically instructs us not to adorn ourselves with precious stones and metals. This teaching forbids ornamental jewelry, whether real or imitation.

Moderation in Cost

Closely associated with the avoidance of ornaments is the principle of moderation in cost. For this reason, we are not to adorn ourselves with gold, pearls, or "costly array." The definition of costly clothing may vary somewhat depending on the culture, society, and income of the individual. A good test is to ask if certain clothing would be an ostentatious display of wealth in the sight of acquaintances and fellow believers. Would it unduly arouse envy? Would it represent good stewardship of the money God has entrusted to our care? Surely it grieves God to see His people buying extravagant clothing, jewelry, and automobiles while they neglect His kingdom and His work suffers in many areas. God has blessed America materially, and He has blessed many Christians financially. He wants us to use our prosperity to support efforts to win the lost and to help the needy, not merely to satisfy our own desires.

Distinction between Male and Female

Deuteronomy 22:5 states another important concept to God: distinction between male and female. Not only are there biological differences between genders, but there are mental and emotional differences as well. In addition, God has established certain social methods for maintaining the distinction between male and female—namely, dress and hair length. (See chapter 9.) This separation is important to God because He has designed different roles in life for the male and the female. In society, this distinction is an important guard against homosexuality, which God hates. (See chapter 11.) The principle of gender distinction in dress is violated by unisex clothing, by men dressing in a feminine way, and by women dressing in a masculine way.

Many argue that Deuteronomy 22:5 does not apply today. Some say that since both sexes wore robes in Bible days there was no clear distinction. While it is true that both wore robes, it is also true that there were clear differences in the types of robes worn by males and those worn by females. This fact is evident from a study of the history and culture of the Middle East as well as from the existence of this teaching in Deuteronomy.

Another objection is that Deuteronomy 22:5 is part of the law given to Israel and does not concern us as Christians. For instance, today we do not literally obey verses 9-11, which prohibit mixing of seed when sowing, plowing with an ox and a donkey yoked together, and weaving wool and linen together in one garment.

To answer this objection, we must rightly divide the Word of God by looking at what these verses are intended to teach us. Verse 5 teaches the distinction of gender, which is a moral law. It was not instituted just for Israel, but it originated with creation and is still relevant today. Verses 9-11 teach the principle of separation, using physical objects as types of spiritual separation. Today, we do not obey the ceremonial aspects of the law as found in verses 9-11, but we do fulfill them in typology. Our separation today is not between kinds of seeds, animals, and fibers but between holy and unholy, spiritual and carnal.

We clearly see the difference in the two types of law, moral and ceremonial, in this chapter because verse 5 uses the word *abomination* but verses 9-11 do not. Specifically, verse 5 says that it is an "abomination unto the LORD thy God" for a person to wear clothes pertaining to the opposite sex. An abomination is something hated or detested, so verse 5 speaks of something that God hates.

God does not change in His likes and dislikes, for He has declared, "I am the Lord, I change not" (Malachi 3:6). God has "repented," or changed His mind, about whether to execute judgment, depending on people's repentance, but His basic character does not change. He is absolute in holiness and in His hatred of sin.

Thus, God's people of all ages must shun what is an abomination to Him. Christians do not need to keep the purely ceremonial part of the Jewish law, for it has been fulfilled in Jesus Christ. (See Colossians 2:16-17.) The ceremonial law did not relate to things God hated but to specific methods of worship and specific marks of identification. In some cases, God designated things as an abomination to Israel—that is, something the Israelites were supposed to hate—but refrained from calling them abominations to Him. As an example, God told Israel that certain animals were abominations to them and unclean to them (Leviticus 11). They were not called abominations to God or to us today. Wearing clothes of the opposite sex is an abomination to God, however, so it is an abomination to God's people of every age. In this connection, we should note that no abomination will enter the New Jerusalem but will be cast into the lake of fire (Revelation 21:8, 27).

The New Testament shows that God still considers distinction of gender to be important. According to I Corinthians 11, men should have short hair while women should have long hair. (See chapter 9.) According to I Corinthians 6:9-10, the "effeminate" will not inherit the kingdom of God. This passage uses two Greek words to describe homosexual activity.

The one translated as "effeminate" is *malakos*, which has the connotation of being soft and effeminate. While the focus is on the sin of homosexuality, part of the problem is that some men act and dress like women.

Not only is Deuteronomy 22:5 timeless, it applies to all cultures. "That which pertaineth unto a man" means clothing traditionally associated with men or patterned after men's clothing. The type of clothing may vary with culture. For example, in Scotland the kilt was traditionally a man's garment, and in some parts of Asia and the Pacific, men wear similar garments. If a certain type of garment has been traditionally and culturally used exclusively by one gender and it is different from similar garments worn by the opposite sex, then it is permissible for the one sex to wear and not for the other sex.

In Western culture, the distinctive clothing of men is pants, and the distinctive clothing of women is dresses and skirts. Although cultural views are changing to allow certain unisex fashions, when Westerners emphasize masculine versus feminine dress they fall back on this distinction. For instance, the doors of public restrooms often have a silhouette of a man in pants and a woman in a dress. The practice of women wearing pants did not gain widespread acceptance in America until World War II. At that time women began to take men's places in factories, as the men went off to war. Around this time, it also became widely accepted for women to cut their hair, smoke cigarettes, and drink alcoholic beverages. When society was disrupted and women assumed men's roles, then it became acceptable for women to wear pants—first for factory work, then for informal occasions, and finally for general public use, including office and church.

Today, most women wear pants sometimes, yet on formal occasions or occasions when they wish to accentuate their femininity, they usually wear dresses. Few men, however, will wear a dress. Indeed, most denominational Christians would disapprove of a man wearing a dress. For example, most would not accept a male pastor who wears a dress in the pulpit. Yet, from the scriptural viewpoint, both actions should be treated in a similar manner.

Although some pants are designed for women, typically they are closely patterned after men's clothing and would still fit under the definition of "that which pertaineth unto a man." "To pertain" means to belong to as a part, attribute, feature, or function; to have reference; to relate. In many cases, women wear styles that are exactly the same as men's styles, such as jeans, military fatigues, and sweat pants. When pants are designed for women, they can be quite form fitting and revealing, and if so they violate the principle of modesty in addition to the key principle of gender distinction.

Separation from the World

Another important principle of outward holiness is separation from the world. God visibly separated the Israelites from the rest of the nations by their food, dress, farming practices, worship ceremonies, and Sabbath rest. It was usually possible to identify Jews simply by observing their dress and actions. As a result of their unique identity, the Jews have survived as the only ancient biblical people to maintain their cultural and religious heritage.

The Egyptians today do not have the same culture, religion, or language as in the days of the pharaohs. The Persians, Syrians, Greeks, and Romans do not have their ancient cultural, religious, and political systems. Most other tribes and nations that coexisted with Israel—such as the Hittites, Babylonians, Edomites, Assyrians, Philistines, and Ammonites—have not even survived as distinct nations. Yet the Jews have maintained their cultural identity through Babylonian captivity, Roman occupation, and nineteen hundred years without a homeland. The reason is that God's laws separated them from other nations and preserved their identity.

Similarly, for Christians to exist as a chosen people, they must have points of separation, both external and internal. In relation to dress and adornment, God has not given us arbitrary commands, but He has chosen points of distinction that also achieve His other objectives of modesty, moderation, humility, and gender differentiation. Consequently, Christian guidelines for conduct and dress help us remain separate from the world around us. They help distance us from temptation and sin, and they help us maintain our identity.

Because of this principle of separation, Christians sometimes avoid certain activities, hairstyles, and clothing that do not violate specific scriptural statements but nevertheless are closely associated with worldly attitudes and behavior. In another culture and time they might be permissible, but if they identify us with an ungodly lifestyle in our society, then we avoid them. For instance, if a certain style of adornment or dress is closely associated with sexual promiscuity, homosexuality, or pagan religion, then Christians avoid it. As an example, the hippies of the 1960s used their hair and dress to express rebellion and sexual permissiveness, so Christians avoided looking like them. Similarly, the communist Chinese used unisex Mao suits as a symbol of their political and social views.

We must exercise caution in following the latest fads and fashions of the world. It is not wrong to follow fashions as long as they are consistent with biblical principles. However, we do not want to become closely identified with a worldly spirit, nor do we want to get caught up in a spirit of competition. Instead, we want to be examples of modesty, moderation, humility, and holiness.

Our dress should be appropriate to the occasion. Good taste and custom can guide us in this matter. When finances prohibit someone from being well dressed, there is certainly no question of holiness. We should not treat a poorly dressed person any different from a rich, well-dressed person, but we should be kind and accepting of both (James 2:1-9). Even in cases of poverty, however, Christians can strive to be clean and neat. We are ambassadors of Christ, so we should represent Him as well as possible.

In short, our outward appearance tells others much about our lifestyle, beliefs, and attitudes. We should ask if our appearance is a good witness of Christianity. Does it identify us with rebellion? Could it be a stumbling block to others? Or is it an example of godliness both to unbelievers and believers?

Makeup

Christian woman are encouraged to adorn themselves—that is, to present themselves as neat, clean, and attractive—but they must do so with "shamefacedness and sobriety" (I Timothy 2:9). "Shamefacedness" means respect, reverence, self-restraint, modesty, or bashfulness toward men; not being bold or forward.

Colored makeup and tattoos are contrary to the principle of avoiding personal ornamentation and vanity. Makeup is obviously designed to attract the opposite sex. It does so by accentuating sensuality in the woman and arousing lust in the man. The application of makeup is not arbitrary, but much of it originated as an imitation of a woman's appearance during sexual arousal. Thus, both in the Old Testament and throughout history, painting the face is associated with brazenness, forwardness, seduction, and prostitution.

According to history, painting of the eyelids to enhance sexual appeal was first introduced in ancient Egypt about 3000 BC. Proverbs 6:25 refers to this practice: "Lust not after her beauty in thine heart; neither let her take thee with her eyelids." The surrounding verses speak of this woman as "evil," "strange," "whorish," and an "adulteress."

A prominent example occurs in II Kings 9:30. Jehu was anointed king of Israel and given the mission of destroying the family of Ahab, who hated God's Word. Jezebel, the wife of Ahab, heard that Jehu was coming and tried to seduce him in order to save her own life. As a means of enticing him, she painted her face or eyes and adorned her head. When Jehu arrived, he discerned her strategy and ordered her to be killed.

Esther, the woman who saved her nation, stands in sharp contrast to Jezebel. The young women who appeared before the Persian king made preparations with oils and perfumes. When they went before the king, they could ask for anything else that they wanted to assist them, and no doubt they chose various cosmetics and ornaments. When Esther's turn came, she asked for nothing but relied on the advice of the king's chamberlain who had charge of the women. (See Esther 2:13-15.) She wanted to be accepted for who she was, and she relied on the will of the Lord.

In Jeremiah 4:30, God compared the backslidden nation of Judah to a woman who tried to appeal to her lovers with makeup and ornaments. Ezekiel 23:36-44 similarly describes Samaria and Jerusalem (the capitals of Israel and Judah) as two women who adorned themselves with makeup and jewelry in order to commit adultery with a variety of lovers. In both cases, God associated makeup with sexual immorality. Nowhere does the Bible associate makeup with a virtuous woman.

In American society before the twentieth century, women generally did not wear makeup, and those who did were considered to be immoral. According to *Encyclopedia Britannica*, it was not until after World War I that makeup became generally acceptable, and even then its use was limited until after World War II. Most conservative churches did not approve of it until that time. Of course, most women today who wear makeup do not have the intention of being immoral but are simply conforming to culture. Nevertheless, these passages of Scripture reveal what God thinks about ornamental makeup. When we abstain from makeup and tattoos, we please Him.

Ornamental Jewelry

Wearing ornamental jewelry violates the principle of avoiding personal ornamentation and the principle of moderation in cost. Under the inspiration of the Holy Spirit, both the apostle Paul and the apostle Peter addressed this aspect of adornment. "To adorn" means to decorate, ornament, beautify, or embellish. According to I Timothy 2:9-10, women are to adorn themselves in modest clothing and with good works, but not with "broided hair, or gold, or pearls, or costly array." Similarly, I Peter 3:3-4 says their adorning should be with "the hidden man of the heart, in that which is not corruptible, even the ornament of a meek and quiet spirit, which is in the sight of God of great price"; it should not be "that outward adorning of plaiting the hair, and of wearing of gold, or of putting on of apparel."

These two passages support each other. Both warn against braided or plaited hair, which refers to the elaborate hair arrangement of that time, particularly to the intertwining of pearls and gold thread in the hair. Both warn against ornamental jewelry, both using the example of a precious metal and one using the example of a precious stone. Both warn against extravagant clothing; the "outward adorning . . . of putting on of apparel" in I Peter refers to clothing worn as excessive ornamentation instead of for practical reasons of modesty and protection from the elements.

While the foregoing New Testament passages provide the most complete and relevant teaching on adornment for

Christians today, God sought to introduce similar principles in the Old Testament.

In Exodus 33:1-11, the Israelites had just sinned by making a golden calf and worshiping it. God had promised to lead them personally into the land of Canaan, but His justice now compelled Him not to appear in their midst lest He consume them. In His mercy, God promised to send an angel to lead them instead. When the people heard this, they began to mourn. As a sign of their sorrow and their repentance, they did not put on their ornaments. The Lord told them they were a stubborn people and instructed, "Put off thy ornaments from thee." In response, they "stripped themselves of their ornaments." They needed to strip themselves of their vanity in the presence of God.

Moses then walked toward the Tabernacle, and all the people stood in the doors of their tents to watch. As a result of their consecration, the Lord came down in a cloud of glory. All the people worshiped Him, and He talked to Moses as a friend. The stripping of unnecessary ornaments had demonstrated that the Israelites really wanted the presence of God. It was a lesson in self-denial and humility. Likewise, if we want the fullness of God's presence and a close relationship with Him as a body of believers, we need to make this type of consecration.

Isaiah 3:16-26 describes the vanity of wearing ornaments. The nation of Judah had become proud, which displeased God. Consequently, He said He would remove all their ornaments. The passage lists the ornaments and expensive apparel that displayed their pride. (Definitions are from Strong's *Concordance* or from the New King James Version where indicated.) They were tinkling ornaments for the feet, cauls (netting for the hair), round tires like the moon (round pendants for the neck, or "crescents" in NKJV), chains (pendants for the ear), bracelets, mufflers (long veils), bonnets (headdresses), ornaments for the legs, headbands, tablets ("perfume boxes" in NKJV), earrings (or "charms" in NKJV), rings, nose jewels, changeable suits of apparel ("festal apparel" in NKJV), mantles (cloaks), wimples (wide cloths), crisping pins ("purses" in NKJV), glasses (mirrors), fine linen, hoods (headdresses), veils, and stomachers (figured mantles for holidays). The various garments and the purses were costly and usually were embroidered elaborately. The mirrors and perfume boxes were often hung from the neck or girdle and worn as ornaments. All of these things have the potential for vanity, and in this case the primary reason for wearing them was pride.

From the foregoing passages in the Old and New Testaments, we learn that our appearance and dress should display humility, modesty, and moderation. We should not wear ornamental jewelry or costly, extravagant clothing. In making decisions about what is appropriate, we should ask, Is this item flashy or gaudy? What is my motive for wearing it? Does it serve a useful purpose? Even if it serves a useful purpose, is it extravagant? Should I consider a less extravagant or less showy alternative? Is God asking me to make a consecration in this area so that I can draw closer to Him?

For example, earrings, necklaces, and bracelets are exclusively ornamental, while a watch is primarily functional rather than ornamental. Even a watch could become ostentatious and vain, however.

If possible, Christians should dress well and in good taste. It is often advisable to spend a greater amount of money for clothing of higher quality, yet we can do so without dressing ostentatiously. Most often, those who are simply and tastefully dressed are the most elegant.

Leaders should carefully consider these teachings and develop personal convictions based on Scripture. They should recognize that their choices in this area will influence others. Indeed, the rest of the congregation will tend to take more liberties than the leaders. Thus, if leaders wear a small item of jewelry that they think is acceptable, followers will tend to wear larger items that are questionable or unacceptable. It is advisable, therefore, for leaders to be somewhat stricter on themselves than what they might expect the congregation to be. When in doubt, all Christians, and especially leaders, should choose alternatives that lead to greater consecration and holiness rather than to the possibility of greater worldliness.

Guidelines for Children

The Bible says, "Train up a child in the way he should go: and when he is old, he will not depart from it" (Proverbs 22:6). We should teach holiness to our children. In choosing and allowing their dress, we should implement the principles of modesty, not using personal ornaments, moderation in cost, distinction between male and female, and separation from the world. Before puberty, modesty is not as significant an issue. Some types of clothing that would be immodest on adults are not immodest on children. Nevertheless, we should not dress children in seductive or provocative styles, as this would be inappropriate and would establish a detrimental precedent for when they grow older.

A Witness in Early Church History

It is interesting to note that despite differences of doctrine and the influx of false doctrines, Christians of the second and third centuries generally continued to adhere to scriptural teachings on adornment and dress. For example, in the third century AD, Tertullian wrote a treatise entitled *On Female Dress*. In it, he taught against rouge, hair dye, wigs, elaborate hair styling for men and women, eyeliner, jewels, and ornaments. He called Christians to temperance and sacrifice. He said that if God treats lust like fornication, then He will not fail to punish those who deliberately arouse lust in others by their dress. He also noted that the person who is accustomed to luxury, jewels, and ornaments will not be willing to sacrifice all, including life itself, for the cause of Christ.

Throughout church history, many revivalists and reformers advocated similar teachings concerning adornment and dress, including the Anabaptists, John Calvin (Reformed leader), John Wesley (Methodist leader), the Holiness movement, and the Pentecostal movement.

The Challenge Today

The final decision rests with us. Will we retain biblical teachings on modesty, humility, and moderation in outward appearance? Will we maintain distinction of the sexes and separation from the world? Or will we succumb to the pressures of the world and its so-called modernization, which is really a revival of ancient evils? Will we identify with God or with the world? May God help us to uphold the complete message of holiness. May God help us to keep the landmarks established by the Word of God, the teaching of our spiritual forefathers, and the leading of the Spirit.

9

Bible Truths Concerning Hair

"If a man have long hair, it is a shame unto him[.] But if a woman have long hair, it is a glory to her: for her hair is given her for a covering" (I Corinthians 11:14-15).

Just as the Bible provides direction for how we can dress in a way that glorifies God, it also directs in how the way we wear our hair can be an act of worship. We find the New Testament teaching about hair in I Corinthians 11:1-16. This passage teaches that a woman should have long, uncut hair and a man should have short hair. At the outset, let us briefly summarize the reasons for this teaching.

Reasons Why a Woman Should Have Long Hair

1. Long hair is a sign of her submission to authority.
2. The angels are watching to see if she has this sign.
3. It is a shame for a woman to pray or prophesy with an uncovered head, for she thereby dishonors her head (leadership). Long hair is her symbolic head covering. If she shears (cuts) her hair it is like shaving her head.

4. Nature teaches her to have long hair as opposed to shorn (cut) hair or a shaved head.
5. Long hair is a woman's glory.
6. It is one of God's methods for maintaining a distinction between male and female.

Reasons Why a Man Should Have Short Hair

1. Short hair on a man is a symbol of leadership and his submission to Christ's leadership.
2. A man who prays or prophesies with his head covered by long hair dishonors his head (leadership), which is Christ.
3. Nature teaches him to have short hair.
4. Long hair is a shame on a man.
5. It is one of God's methods for maintaining a distinction between male and female.

To fully understand and appreciate these reasons, we need to look at the significance of hair in the Old Testament. The Old Testament was written for our learning, example, and admonition (Romans 15:4; I Corinthians 10:11). The law served as a schoolmaster to bring people to Christ (Galatians 3:24). The Old Testament contains many types and shadows that help us to appreciate and understand the meaning of the New Testament (Colossians 2:16-17; Hebrews 8:5; 10:1).

Hair in the Old Testament

Hair was a symbol of perfection and strength. Among the Jews, an abundance of hair indicated perfection and strength. Lack of hair symbolized the opposite: imperfection, lost glory, and powerlessness. For example, the young men in II Kings 2:23 contemptuously called Elisha a bald head. This expression did not necessarily indicate actual baldness but meant that the person so called was worthless, imperfect, and without glory.

Cutting of hair was a symbol of disgrace or mourning. Throughout the Old Testament, the cutting of hair symbolized disgrace (Ezra 9:3; Nehemiah 13:25) or mourning (Isaiah 22:12; Ezekiel 27:31; 29:18; Micah 1:16). The loss of hair signified barrenness, sin, and the judgment of God (Isaiah 3:17, 24; 15:2; Jeremiah 47:5; 48:37; Ezekiel 7:18; Amos 8:10). In Isaiah 3:17-24, the judgment pronounced on proud women was that instead of having well-set hair they would be struck bald by God. In essence, they would be without honor and would be ashamed. In Jeremiah 7:29, God used cut hair as a symbol of Judah's backslidden condition and her rejection by God.

Hair was a symbol of glory. A woman's long hair symbolizes the blessings of God in Ezekiel 16:7. Gray hair is a crown of glory (Proverbs 16:31). God told Ezekiel to cut his hair as an object lesson of God's judgment on Judah (Ezekiel 5:1-4, 12). He then showed Ezekiel that His glory would depart from the Temple in Jerusalem (Ezekiel 10:3-10). Ezekiel without hair signified Ezekiel without glory, which in turn symbolized Jerusalem without the glory of God.

Uncut hair was a mark of separation unto God. When we study the vow of the Nazarites (or, more accurately, Nazirites), we discover that hair could be a mark of separation (Numbers 6:1-21). According to Strong's Concordance this name comes from the Hebrew *nazir*, which means "separate, i.e. consecrated." The Nazarites were separated unto Jehovah as shown by three outward signs. A Nazarite was not to partake of grapes or any product of grapes, was not to touch a corpse, and was not to cut the hair on the head. This last sign was the only one that immediately identified a Nazarite by outward appearance.

Either a man or a woman could be a Nazarite (verse 2). The Nazarite vow could be taken for a temporary period or for a lifetime. Paul took temporary vows, while Samson was a Nazarite from his mother's womb (Acts 21:20-27; Judges 13:7). Since abundance of hair signified strength, perfection, and glory, the free growth of hair on the head represented the dedication of all one's strength and power to God. The hair was "the consecration of his God upon his head" (Numbers 6:7).

The Nazarites could not cut their hair at all, but they let it grow. During their period of separation they were holy. At the end of the vow they cut their hair (verse 5). The reason they could not defile themselves by touching a corpse was that the mark of their separation was on their head for all to see (verse 7). If Nazarites broke their vow by becoming defiled, they had to shave their head (verse 9). The reason is that their long hair would signify that they were still separated, while their actions proved otherwise. Their appearance and actions would be in conflict.

If Nazarites broke their vow, they had to begin all over again (verse 12). Their prior commitment was not counted if the vow was broken. (See also Ezekiel 3:20; 18:24; 33:12-13.) When the vow was completed, their hair was cut and put on the altar for a peace offering (verse 18). It was called the hair of separation unto God (verse 19).

Each seventh year in Israel was called a sabbatical year. Trees and vines were not pruned, and fields were not plowed or sown. In particular, grape vines were left undressed (Leviticus 25:5, 11). In Hebrew, the word "undressed" is *nazir*, the same word translated as "Nazarite" in Numbers. In fact, a second definition of this word is "an unpruned vine (like an unshorn Nazarite)." These "Nazarite" vines were not cut or pruned but were allowed to grow freely, just like the Nazarites' hair.

In summary, in the Old Testament hair was often a symbol of power, perfection, and glory. The absence of hair could signify worthlessness and glory departed. Christians today are not Nazarites in the literal sense, but our study has shown that the hair of the Nazarites was a visible mark of separation from the world and consecration to God.

New Testament Teaching

We now turn to the New Testament teaching on hair as found in I Corinthians 11:1-16. Most denominational churches ignore this passage, concluding that it does not apply today. Some interpret it to mean that women must pray with some type of cloth on their heads. Most conservative churches at one time taught women to have long hair, and some continue to do so today.

Since all Scripture is given by the inspiration of God (II Timothy 3:16), we should not ignore any passage of Scripture, for each is precious and important. We should especially heed instructions to the New Testament church, for we are part of that church. Let us analyze this passage of Scripture in that light.

Verses 1-2. Paul admonished believers to follow him and to keep the ordinances or teachings that he had delivered to them. Among these ordinances is his teaching concerning hair in the subsequent verses.

Verse 3. God is the head of Christ. As a human, Jesus submitted to the eternal Spirit of God that dwelt in Him, thereby setting an example for us. Christ subjected His flesh to the plan and purpose of God, even unto death (Philippians 2:8).

Similarly, Christ is the head of the man, and the man is the head of the woman. God intends for the man to be the leader of the family. He is to be the spiritual representative of the home. In the beginning, God held Adam primarily accountable for human sinfulness. The sins of fathers particularly affect children (Exodus 20:5). Moreover, a woman is to respect the leadership of her own husband (Ephesians 5:22; Colossians 3:18; I Peter 3:1).

Verse 4. A man should not have his head covered when he prays or prophesies. If he does, he dishonors his head or leader, namely, Christ. Prophesying includes any anointed preaching and testimony.

Verse 5. A woman who prays or prophesies (including preaching and testimony) with her head uncovered dishonors her head or leader, which is the man. In other words, the sexes should not try to change places. The woman's covering is a sign of her role in God's plan. According to verse 15, long hair is the symbolic covering that God has given her, and according to verse 6 it should be unshorn or uncut.

Verse 6. If a woman is not going to cover her head (by letting her hair grow long), then this is equivalent to cutting off her hair. But this is a disgrace or a shame to her. It signifies the taking away of her glory in God's sight. Since it is a shame for her hair to be shorn (cut) or shaved, she should be covered (let her hair grow long).

Verses 7-9. Adam was created in the image of God and subsequently Eve was also (Genesis 1:26-27). The man is the representative of the family before God, with the authority and responsibility to provide for his family, protect his family, and lead his family spiritually. As a sign of his position, his head should not be covered (with long hair, verse 14). The woman originally came from the man (Genesis 2:22). She is his partner, a helper comparable to him (Genesis 2:20), who respects his position and follows his godly leadership. Woman is the crowning glory of man. To demonstrate this relationship, her head should be covered (verse 6) with her glory, which is her long hair (verse 15). In short, male and female are equally important in God's plan, but their roles are distinct, and God wants this distinction to be displayed and preserved outwardly by their hair.

Verse 10. The angels are involved with this subject, as they observe the obedience or disobedience of humans to God's plan. The angels desire to look into our salvation (I

Peter 1:12). Pride and rebellion caused the fall of Satan and many angels (I Timothy 3:6; Isaiah 14:12-15). Thus, a woman should have "power" on her head as an example to the angels. The Greek word here is *exousia*, meaning "authority," and in this context it indicates a mark or sign of authority. The angels look to see if women have the sign of consecration, submission, and power with God, or if they are rebellious like Satan. Women's hair shows the angels whether or not the church is submissive to Christ, the head of the church.

Verses 11-12. Women are not inferior to men, and men are not complete without women. Both depend on each other. This principle of complementarity and interdependence is especially true in the church. The roles are different, however, and God has designated the man to be the leader of the family.

Verse 13. Paul used a question as a part of his teaching method. Is it proper for a woman to pray to God uncovered? His answer is no; it is a shame for her to do so (verse 5).

Verse 14. Nature, not just custom, teaches a man to have short hair but a woman to have long hair. Since God is the Creator of nature, the teaching of nature in this situation comes from God. God's purpose is to make a distinction of gender in this area.

Verse 15. A woman's hair is given for her glory and for a covering to satisfy the requirements of the preceding verses. This verse does not mention any other covering such as a hat or scarf. It would be difficult for a woman to put on a scarf every time she prays or witnesses to someone, especially if she prays without ceasing (I Thessalonians 5:17). This verse explains that a woman does not have to wear a veil of cloth; her hair is sufficient covering.

The Greek word for "have long hair" here is *komaō*, which means "wear long hair, let one's hair grow long" or "wear tresses of hair." The word for "covered" in verse 6 is *katakaluptō*, meaning "to cover wholly, i.e., to veil." The word for "covering" in verse 15 is *peribolaion*, which is "something thrown around one, i.e., a mantle, veil." Thus, verses 5-6 teach that a woman's head should be covered wholly or veiled. Verse 15 says her hair is a mantle or veil; it is a symbolic article of apparel for the head. Clearly, long hair is the covering that meets the requirements of verses 5, 6, and 13.

Verse 16. The people of God are not contentious. The church has no custom of being contentious over the teachings of God's Word. It has no custom regarding hair other than what Paul had just described. Some say this verse means that if anyone disagrees with these teachings, obedience is not required. If this were true, however, Paul's entire teaching in this section would be in vain, and he would be condoning contention and disobedience. Paul would not say, "If you do not have such a custom, then you are not required to obey the Word of God and the ordinances of the church." Reading verses 2 and 16 together, the message is that we should obey these teachings instead of being contentious.

Reasons for Biblical Teaching on Hair

Hair symbolizes the relationship of husband and wife, which in turn represents the Lord's relationship with the church. A woman's long hair symbolizes that she submits to God's plan and to the family leadership of her husband. It is her glory. It is a sign to the angels of her commitment to God and her power with God. It is a covering so that she can pray and prophesy publicly without being ashamed. Similarly, a man's short hair symbolizes that he submits to God's plan and accepts the family leadership position.

Nature teaches women to let their hair grow long and men to cut their hair short. First, nature teaches that there should be a visible distinction between male and female. Second, in almost all cultures, men have worn short hair in comparison to women. Third, men are ten times more likely to go bald than women. It is natural for a man not to have any hair but unnatural for a woman not to have hair. Therefore, when men and women follow the biblical teaching on hair, they follow God's plan as established in creation. Hair length makes a gender distinction, which God considers to be important. (See Deuteronomy 22:5.) It is also a mark of separation from the world. (See chapter 8.)

God always gives us a choice to do His will or not. He never forces us to be what He wants us to be. We did not choose to be male or female, however; that choice was determined for us at conception. By our choice of dress and hairstyle, we show acceptance or rejection of God's plan for us as male or female, husband or wife, father or mother. The roles are equally important in family, church, and society, but they are different. God wants us to demonstrate our willingness to accept the roles He has chosen for us.

The relationship between husband and wife is like that between Christ and the church. The husband is the head of the wife as Christ is head of the church (Ephesians 5:22-23). Therefore, when Christian men and women demonstrate their acceptance of God's plan by their hair, they also demonstrate the church's submission to Christ.

How Long Is Long?

Our study of the Nazarites indicates that long hair as a mark of separation means uncut hair or hair that is allowed to grow freely. By letting the hair grow freely, women allow nature, the teacher that Paul appealed to in I Corinthians 11:14, to determine the proper length for each individual. The Greek word for long hair in verse 15 means that a woman should let her hair grow long. Moreover, verse 6 indicates that if a woman cuts her hair, it is the same as if she shaves her head. The Bible does not provide any other definition for long hair on women, nor does it designate any particular measurement as long. The point is not to grow it to a certain length, because different individuals' hair naturally grows to different lengths. If a woman does not cut her hair, then it is long in God's sight. Finally, the fundamental principle is that a woman's hair needs to be visibly longer than that of men.

A man's hair should be at least short enough to distinguish him from women. This length may vary somewhat in various ages and cultures. In determining the appropriate length of a man's hair we should consider the following questions. Is it shorter than that of the average woman in our society? Is it a good witness, or is it a reproach to the church and to Christ? Is it a sign of rebellion against authority in the community or in the church? Is it a stumbling block or an offense to other members of the church? (See I Corinthians 8:9-13.) Does it identify him with elements of the world from which he has been saved?

Under certain cultural circumstances, all but the first of these questions could apply to facial hair also. Whether shaved or allowed to grow, a man's beard is a sign of masculinity. In general, facial hair was highly regarded in the Bible and in many other times and cultures, but in white, middle-class America of the 1960s it became a sign of rebellion. In the Bible, we find positive examples both of shaving and growing beards. (See Genesis 41:14; Psalm 133:2.)

The notion that Jesus had long, womanly hair is a myth. He was not a Nazarite as some believe, but a Nazarene, which means an inhabitant of the city of Nazareth. He drank the fruit of the vine and touched corpses, so He did not have a Nazarite vow. The art that shows Him with long hair was painted many centuries later and is without scriptural or historical foundation. It reflects medieval rather than biblical customs. Roman sculpture and coinage as well as other historical sources show that men generally wore short hair in Christ's day. In any case, He would not have worn womanly hair in contradiction to the Word of God.

Attitudes

There are two concerns regarding a woman's attitude toward long hair. Some may resent the need to care for and fix long hair. But with moderate effort it is possible to fix long hair so that it looks modern, neat, and attractive. Many promise to do anything for the Lord, yet when it comes to long hair, they are unwilling to make the effort. Since God has made His wishes clear, disobeying Him demonstrates self-centeredness, a lack of consecration, and a lack of love.

Another danger is pride. It is possible to take the very hair that is supposed to be a sign of submission and arrange it in an ostentatious display. Overly elaborate hairdos and extravagant hairpieces draw attention to self rather than the message of the long hair. Such ostentation undermines the purpose and testimony of the long hair. Many people have been impressed with the beautiful, holy, long hair of Christian women, but others have been perplexed, confused, and repelled by showy displays.

Thus I Timothy 2:9 warns women not to adorn themselves with "broided hair," which, according to the Amplified Bible, includes "[elaborate] hair arrangement." We find the same admonition in I Peter 3:3. Both verses refer to elaborate hair arrangement in the first century, such as braiding the hair with a string of pearls or with gold coins attached to silk cords. We must exercise moderation and temperance in all things, including hair arrangement. It would be a shame for a woman to undermine the message of holiness with something intended to be a sign of holiness.

Shall We Obey I Corinthians 11:1-16?

We cannot treat this passage casually, merely because we think it is outdated or inconvenient. If we ignore it, then what is to prevent us from ignoring the teaching about communion in the same chapter or any other passage of Scripture?

Some may consider disobedience in this matter to be a minor thing. No doubt Moses thought it was a minor thing to disobey God by striking a rock to obtain water instead of speaking to the rock. After all, he had stricken a rock to obtain water once before at God's command. Yet God did not allow him to enter the Promised Land because he did not obey His instruction to speak to the rock on the second occasion. (See Exodus 17:6; Numbers 20:7-12.) In God's plan, the rock represented Christ (I Corinthians 10:4), who was smitten once for us and whose grace is now available whenever we simply speak His name in faith. Although Moses had no way of understanding this significance, he should have simply obeyed God's plan, and he paid a severe price for not doing so. It is always important to obey God's Word in all things.

Regardless of personal inconvenience or the opinions of others, it is our responsibility and privilege to serve God. Doing so is the very definition of true love. Jesus said, "If you love me, keep my commandments" (John 14:15).

Session 5

Discussion Questions

1. Multiple principles must be considered when choosing apparel. Describe your process for deciding if clothes fit within your commitment to holiness.

2. Do you think apparel and adornment send a message to people around us? If so, how should that factor into the choices we make about dress?

3. How is hair a sign of glory?

4. Describe how hair reflects our relationship with God and within the family.

5. What do you think your apparel, adornment, and hair testify to the people around you?

Session 6

10

The Temple of God

"What? know ye not that your body is the temple of the Holy Ghost which is in you? . . . If any man defile the temple of God, him shall God destroy" (I Corinthians 6:19; 3:17).

In our commitment to worship the Lord in the beauty of holiness (Psalms 96:9), we are careful with how we treat the body God has given us. The body is a temple, or dwelling place, for the Spirit of God. For this reason, we are not to defile the body but are to keep it holy. In the broadest application, we are not to commit sin with our physical bodies, and we are to protect the collective body of Christ, which is the church. In this chapter, we will restrict our discussion to specific activities that harm and defile our physical bodies. We will particularly discuss the application of these principles to food, alcoholic beverages, tobacco, and drugs.

Food

Immediately after the Creation, God gave to humans all vegetables, grains, and fruits for food, with the exception of the tree of knowledge of good and evil (Genesis 1:29; 2:16-17). After the Flood, God explained that humans could eat every living thing, both plants and animals, with the exception of blood (Genesis 9:1-4). In both instances, God retained one thing as a symbol of His lordship. While He specified that humans could eat meat, He prohibited them from eating blood because it is a symbol of life and He alone is the giver of life.

The law of Moses restricted the diet of Israel in several ways. (See Leviticus 11; Deuteronomy 14.) God allowed the Israelites to eat all animals that both chewed the cud and had a divided hoof (Leviticus 11:3). Animals forbidden by this rule were the camel, coney, hare, and pig. Aquatic animals without scales and fins were also unclean (Leviticus 11:10). Twenty kinds of birds, mostly scavengers and birds of prey, were unclean (Leviticus 11:13-19). All flying, creeping things—i.e., insects—were unclean with the exception of the locust, the bald locust, the beetle (or cricket, NKJV and NIV), and the grasshopper.

The main purpose of these dietary laws was to separate Israel from all other nations. They also helped to protect the Israelites from unsanitary and disease-carrying food. In those days, medical information about germs was unknown while sanitation was primitive by modern standards, so these laws promoted health. For example, pork is a well-known source of trichinosis if it is not cooked properly.

In Acts 15 the leaders of the New Testament church met to establish which restrictions of the Jewish law apply to Gentiles. The moral teachings were not an issue, because everyone knew that they were the same in every age, but they discussed ceremonial laws such as circumcision. They decided that Gentile Christians did not need to be circumcised but needed to keep four points of the Jewish law:

1. *Abstain from food offered to idols.* We are not to have anything to do with idol worship. We are not to participate in idolatrous festivals or eat food in situations that would give seeming endorsement of idolatry.

2. *Abstain from fornication.* This word covers all types of sexual intercourse outside marriage, including premarital sex, adultery, and homosexuality. (See chapter 11.) This

statement is probably included here to make sure that the Gentiles would define fornication according to the provisions of the law of Moses instead of by pagan beliefs. For instance, the Gentiles needed to know the definition of incest according to the law of Moses (Leviticus 18:6-18).

3. *Abstain from things strangled.* The reference is to Leviticus 17:13-14. When an animal is killed, it must be butchered so that the blood drains out of the carcass. If an animal is merely strangled, the blood remains in it, and anyone who eats the meat would be eating blood, which is forbidden.

4. *Abstain from blood.* As discussed below, we are not to eat blood, because it represents life. This command teaches us that life is sacred, and therefore we should abstain from bloodshed—the taking of human life.

Acts 15 does not mention any of the Jewish laws concerning unclean animals. Consequently, Christians are free to eat anything except for blood and, in certain situations, food offered to idols. The Old Testament laws concerning food were a shadow of things to come. They signify Christians' need to distinguish between clean and unclean things in a moral sense and to separate themselves from everything that is spiritually unclean. But Christians are not bound by the specific dietary laws of Moses. "Let no man therefore judge you in meat, or in drink, . . . which are a shadow of things to come; but the body is of Christ" (Colossians 2:16-17).

In the last days some teachers will start "forbidding to marry, and commanding to abstain from meats, which God hath created to be received with thanksgiving of them which believe and know the truth" (I Timothy 4:3). Such teaching against marriage and against certain types of food is contrary to the will of God. Marriage is sanctified by the Word of God, and all foods are sanctified by thanksgiving and prayer (verses 4-5). There is no New Testament restriction on certain kinds of food.

Temperance and Gluttony

Christians are to be temperate and moderate in their eating habits. We should practice good eating habits to preserve our health and strength, and we should refrain from foods that affect us adversely.

We should not be guilty of gluttony—eating to excess. Excessive eating can be sinful (Deuteronomy 21:20; Proverbs 23:21). Proverbs 25:16 teaches us to be temperate and moderate in eating. Jesus warned us not to be "overcharged with surfeiting," which includes eating excessively or to the point of nausea (Luke 21:34). Some people refuse to drink alcohol or smoke cigarettes because these substances are harmful to the body, but they literally eat themselves to death. Overeating and improper eating can cause a variety of diseases and eventually a premature death.

This is an abuse of the temple of God. What impression do we make on sinners if we condemn intemperance and overindulgence in some areas while being equally guilty in the area of eating? What kind of image do ministers present if they are grossly overweight from too much eating and too little exercise? We have Christian liberty in the area of food, but we must also follow our common sense and the leading of the Spirit.

We are to be "temperate in all things" (I Corinthians 9:25). Temperance means moderation and self-control. It should be our watchword when we consider any physical activity or fleshly emotion. Those who rule their spirit are better than those who conquer a city (Proverbs 16:32). Those who do not rule their spirit are like a city without defenses (Proverbs 25:28). We must keep our bodies under subjection (I Corinthians 9:27). We must not yield our bodies to anything but the Spirit of God (Romans 6:12-13).

For these reasons, we abstain from anything that would cause us to lose control of ourselves or remove us from the guidance of the Holy Spirit, either permanently by addiction or temporarily by intoxication. Paul explained the proper exercise of Christian liberty in this matter: "All things are lawful unto me, but all things are not expedient [beneficial, helpful]: all things are lawful for me, but I will not be brought under the power of any" (I Corinthians 6:12). If we yield ourselves to something, then we become its servant (Romans 6:16). If we allow ourselves to become addicted or intoxicated, then we undermine our defense against sin, and God cannot use us as He wills.

Beverages

The law was lenient concerning drinks (Deuteronomy 14:26), yet the Old Testament warns against intoxicating drinks (Proverbs 20:1; Isaiah 5:11). The New Testament says that whatever we eat or drink, we should do it for the glory of God (I Corinthians 10:31). In considering what to eat or drink, we should ask, "Can I eat or drink this to the glory of God?"

Coffee, tea, and most carbonated beverages are mild stimulants because they contain caffeine. Medical research reveals that under normal circumstances caffeine is not harmful. However, if we become nervous, irritable, weak, sick, or unable to fast unless we get our morning cup of coffee or our daily soft drink, then we should carefully evaluate our use. We do not need any habit that controls or dictates to us. If any substance causes harmful side effects or is habit forming, we must learn to control it.

Alcoholic Beverages

With the principle of self-control in mind, we must give special attention to alcohol: "Wine is a mocker, strong drink is raging: and whosoever is deceived thereby is not wise" (Proverbs 20:1). "Look not thou upon the wine when it is red, when it giveth his colour in the cup, when it moveth itself aright" (Proverbs 23:31). This statement is a clear warning against drinking wine after it has fermented and has become intoxicating. The evil consequences of drinking wine and mixed wine are woe, sorrow, contention, babbling, wounds, bloodshot eyes, sexual sin, indecent talk, loss of balance and coordination, insensibility, and addiction (Proverbs 23:29-35). Additionally, lovers of wine will not be rich (Proverbs 21:17).

Throughout the Old Testament, all who were separated to God were forbidden to drink wine and strong drink. Nazarites were prohibited from drinking alcoholic beverages (Numbers 6:3; Judges 13:7). John the Baptist did not drink it (Luke 1:15). It was not for kings and princes lest it cause them to forget God's law and pervert justice (Proverbs 31:4-5). Priests were forbidden to drink it when they ministered before God in the Tabernacle or Temple (Leviticus 10:9; Ezekiel 44:21).

As Christians, all of us are separated unto God. We are kings and priests, a royal priesthood, and living sacrifices unto God (Revelation 1:6; I Peter 2:9; Romans 12:1). Our special identity indicates that we should not drink alcoholic beverages.

Sin resulted from the first wine drinking recorded in the Bible. When Noah became drunk, he dishonored his own body, causing embarrassment to others and an opportunity for others to sin (Genesis 9:20-25). When Lot became intoxicated, he committed incest with his own daughters (Genesis 19:32-38). God pronounced a woe on drunkenness (Isaiah 5:11). Strong drink caused the people, the priests, and the prophets to err, to lose their way, and to lose their spiritual eyesight (Isaiah 28:7). Wine enslaves the heart of people, just as harlotry does (Hosea 4:11). God also pronounced a woe on those who give drink to their neighbors (Habakkuk 2:15).

The New Testament classifies drunkenness as a sin that will keep people from inheriting the kingdom of God (I Corinthians 6:10; Galatians 5:19-21). Jesus, Paul, and Peter all warned against drunkenness (Luke 21:34; Romans 13:13; Ephesians 5:18; I Peter 4:3). Bishops, deacons, and aged women are specifically instructed not to be given to wine (I Timothy 3:3, 8; Titus 1:7; 2:3).

After reviewing the teaching of Scripture, we conclude that Christians should not indulge in alcoholic beverages. Some biblical references seem to support the drinking of wine, however. To study them, we will investigate the Hebrew and Greek words for wine.

Two major Hebrew words are translated "wine" in the Old Testament. Nine other Hebrew words for various types of wine and strong drink appear only a few times. *Yayin* is the most common word. It can mean any type of wine, but it usually refers to fermented wine. Many verses clearly use *yayin* to mean fermented wine (Genesis 9:21; 19:32; II Samuel 13:28; Esther 1:10; Proverbs 20:1; 23:31; 31:4). *Yayin* can also refer to freshly made, unfermented grape juice (Isaiah 16:10; Jeremiah 48:33).

The other frequently used Hebrew word for wine is *tiyrosh*. It almost always refers to newly made, unfermented wine. Only this word is used for the wine that was to be tithed, because God wanted tithes first, before significant fermentation took place (Deuteronomy 12:17; 14:23; Nehemiah 13:5). It is the word used for prosperity in the phrase "corn and wine" (Genesis 27:28, 37; Deuteronomy 7:13; etc.). It is translated "new wine" in many places (Proverbs 3:10; Joel 1:10; etc.) and as "sweet wine" in one place (Micah 6:15). Isaiah 65:8 uses *tiyrosh* to speak of "new wine found in the cluster." Here it clearly refers to unfermented grape juice, even juice still in the grape.

The Greek *oinos* is the original word for wine in the New Testament. It usually refers to fermented wine, but like its Hebrew counterparts it can refer to unfermented wine as well. At least three New Testament verses definitely use it in this way (Matthew 9:17; Mark 2:22; Luke 5:37). These verses say that new, unfermented wine is not placed in old wineskins because when the wine ferments it would burst them. The Greek word *gleukos* appears only once, where it is translated "new wine" (Acts 2:13). It can mean freshly made wine (grape juice), or it can mean sweet wine. The latter could be quite intoxicating, as Acts 2 indicates.

In sum, the word *wine* in both testaments can refer to fermented or unfermented grape juice. In New Testament days, wine was often served at meals, but in this case it was greatly diluted with water so that it would not be intoxicating in normal quantities. Moreover, methods of preserving grape juice in an unfermented condition were well known. In light of these facts and the biblical warnings against wine, we should not use biblical references for wine to promote the drinking of strong alcoholic beverages.

People in the Old Testament often drank alcoholic beverages, but we see the detrimental results. They did not have the overcoming power that accompanies the indwelling Holy Spirit. The law showed people how sinful they were but did not give them power over sin. If it had been perfect, there would be no need for the new covenant. Today, God gives us grace and power to overcome. We can and must live up to God's ideal for the church as a body of separated, holy people.

Jesus turned water into wine at a wedding feast in Cana (John 2:1-11). He thereby performed an act of creation, which indicates that the wine was fresh, not fermented, for fermentation is a process of decay. Verse 10 does not say that the guests got drunk but simply that they had freely drunk the other wine provided by the host. In any case, it is not reasonable to suppose that Jesus gave people a strong drink that would enable them to get drunk. Drunkenness is a sin, and God tempts no one to sin (Galatians 5:21; James 1:13).

Paul advised Timothy, "Drink no longer water, but use a little wine for thy stomach's sake and thine often infirmities" (I Timothy 5:23). He recommended that Timothy drink juice instead of water in order to strengthen his body and soothe his weak stomach. Perhaps he was advising Timothy to stay away from the unsanitary local water or to take a small amount of wine for medicinal purposes. He would not have instructed Timothy to drink a strong alcoholic beverage, for that would only aggravate his weakened condition.

The Bible does not say that Jesus and the disciples used "wine" at the Last Supper, but it simply says "the fruit of the vine" (Matthew 26:29; Mark 14:25; Luke 22:18). These words tell us they used juice from the grape without specifying whether it was fermented or not. If it was the typical diluted juice served at meals, then it was not intoxicating. Technically, fresh juice begins to ferment as soon as it is made, unless the process is halted artificially, but in the early stages it is not intoxicating.

Moreover, the same reasons why they used unleavened bread could have led them to use unfermented wine. In this context, leaven symbolizes impurity or sin. Leaven is an agent such as yeast (a type of fungus) that causes the fermentation of bread dough. Chemically, this process is the same type of decay or organic change that causes juice to ferment. The purpose of our discussion is not to prescribe a certain form for the communion service but to show that we cannot use the Last Supper to justify social drinking of alcoholic beverages.

Some Corinthians got drunk at church when partaking of their fellowship meal before the actual communion service (I Corinthians 11:20-22). Each person brought his or her own food (verse 21), and some evidently brought fermented wine. This passage does not condone the practice but condemns it.

In sum, drunkenness is a work of the flesh that will keep people from inheriting the kingdom of God. In addition, both in the Bible and in our day alcohol is the source of many evils. It causes poverty, sickness, lost time, lost money, heartache, violence, evil thoughts, family breakups, sexual sins, physical injuries, mental injuries, and death.

There is no way to measure the sin that alcohol induces, but we can see its effects every day. Surely, these evils are great enough to demonstrate that the warnings of Proverbs 23:29-35 and 21:17 are true.

The biblical and social arguments for abstention from alcoholic beverages are strong. First, it is practically impossible for people to drink so little that they are never affected mentally or never get drunk. Inevitably, their behavior and actions will be affected to some degree. At that point, they are no longer in complete control of themselves and will often do things they should not do. They are no longer able to fully guard themselves against temptation and sin. They become the servant of alcohol when they yield their bodies to it. Since our bodies are the temple of the Holy Spirit, we do not want anything else to gain control of them. Likewise, we do not want to use something that is physically dangerous and debilitating. Either way, we would defile our bodies.

Second, not everyone can resist the temptation presented by a drink, and not everyone can handle even a small amount of alcohol. The safest course is not to touch it at all. Even those who think they can safely handle it can easily create a stumbling block for others. This is a sufficient reason in itself for abstention according to Romans 14:21. Children and teenagers, as well adults who have struggled with alcohol, all benefit from a good example and are harmed by a bad example.

Finally, the Bible tells us to avoid all appearance of evil (I Thessalonians 5:22). We need to consider our reputation within the church and the reputation of the church in the eyes of the world. To some, abstention may seem extreme, but it is a guaranteed solution to all the problems caused by alcohol. Without the Holy Spirit, abstention may seem difficult or impossible, but the Spirit gives us power to overcome. God makes us a new creation with new loves and desires (II Corinthians 5:17). He takes away the very desire so that we no longer want to drink. The Spirit gives us all the joy, peace, relaxation, and satisfaction that we need (Romans 14:17; Ephesians 5:18). Alcohol may give temporary joy and temporary escape from problems, but the Holy Spirit gives us permanent joy and permanent solutions to our problems.

Drugs and Narcotics

Our discussion of the evils of alcohol applies to other drugs as well, for alcohol is a type of drug. Marijuana, for example, causes many of the same evils as alcohol. Its use causes lack of self-control, can cause psychological addiction, and can lead to use of hard drugs. The hard drugs are clearly addictive and physically harmful, and are a major cause of crime. Any recreational drug use that causes the equivalent of drunkenness (loss of self-control), leads to sin, causes physical harm, or causes us to become dependent on it (addiction) is contrary to the will of God. We also need to be cautious with legal medications so as to minimize or avoid these dangers. We should practice moderation, self-control, and self-discipline if we use painkillers, sleeping pills, or other medications.

Tobacco

Tobacco defiles the human body. "To defile" means to dirty, make filthy, dishonor, corrupt the purity or perfection of, contaminate. For centuries, godly leaders have recognized that smoking is filthy and harmful to the body. The Holy Spirit taught them that it was harmful long before science did.

The Bible does not directly refer to tobacco since it was not used in Bible days. It was first used by Native Americans and came to the attention of the world after Europeans discovered America. But the principles of God's Word apply to every age, culture, and country, including circumstances that did not exist in New Testament times. When facing new situations, God leads the church by His Spirit and enables the church to make appropriate decisions and applications of biblical principles. (See Matthew 18:18; Acts 15:28.) Thus, the church body and godly leaders have authority to instruct believers with regard to tobacco and drugs, even though the Bible does not specifically mention them.

Modern science has determined that tobacco is highly addictive and that smoking is harmful to the body. Consequently, U.S. law currently bans cigarette advertising on television. Every package of cigarettes and every printed advertisement for cigarettes must have a message such as the following: "Warning: The Surgeon General Has Determined That Cigarette Smoking Is Dangerous to Your Health." Smoking is the leading cause of lung cancer and emphysema. It is also associated with many other types of cancer and respiratory illnesses as well as strokes and heart trouble. "Tobacco use is the leading preventable cause of death in the United States, resulting in approximately 440,000 deaths each year. More than 8.6 million people in the United States have at least one serious illness caused by smoking."

According to the World Health Organization, smoking is the second major cause of death worldwide. Ten percent of all adult deaths are now caused by tobacco. If current smoking patterns continue, one-half of the people who smoke—about 650 million people in 2006—will eventually die because of tobacco. Tobacco is responsible for 4.1 percent of worldwide disease.

If health experts around the world agree smoking is detrimental, we as Christians should avoid subjecting our temples to it. In addition, tobacco is highly addictive. Many people try to break the habit but simply cannot without God's help. For all these reasons we do not use tobacco in any form.

Conclusion

Because of God's extravagant mercies, we have the honor of being a temple in which His Spirit may dwell. To reverence this special relationship, we should respect our bodies and make our temples habitable: "Let us cleanse ourselves from all filthiness of the flesh and spirit" (II Corinthians 7:1). "Present your bodies a living sacrifice, holy, acceptable unto God, which is your reasonable service" (Romans 12:1).

11

Sexual Relationships

"Thou shalt not commit adultery" (Exodus 20:14).
"Abstain from . . . fornication" (Acts 15:20).

We conclude our study of holiness with attention to how we treat our bodies and how we interact with one another. The Bible is clear in its teaching regarding marriage and sexual relationships. It endorses the marriage of one man and one woman who make a lifelong commitment, and it condemns all sexual relationships outside such a marriage. Numerous passages in both testaments condemn adultery and fornication. Together, these words refer to all extramarital sexual relationships.

Marriage

God instituted marriage in the very beginning by creating Adam and then creating Eve as "a helper comparable to him" (Genesis 2:18, 24, NKJV), or "a helper as his partner" (NRSV). God's purpose in ordaining marriage was to provide for companionship, communion, and partnership between husband and wife and to devise a method of procreation. His plan was for husband and wife to leave their families and form a union with each other (Genesis 2:24). This union was to be heterosexual, lifelong, and monogamous, for God had joined them together.

Although some prominent men in the Old Testament practiced polygamy, this was not God's plan from the beginning. Polygamy was introduced by Lamech, who was also the second recorded murderer (Genesis 4:19, 23). The Bible specifically insists on monogamy for kings, bishops, deacons, and elders (Deuteronomy 17:17; I Timothy 3:2, 12; Titus 1:6). We can conclude, then, that God's plan for marriage was monogamy and a lasting commitment.

As such, God hates divorce (Malachi 2:15-16). In Matthew 19:3-9, some Pharisees tested Jesus by asking Him about divorce. He explained that the law of Moses allowed divorce only because of the hardness of people's hearts. Then He reiterated God's original plan for marriage: "They twain shall be one flesh. . . . What therefore God hath joined together, let not man put asunder."

God created sex as a sacred part of the marriage relationship. He is the one who created male and female and placed an attraction between them. Some traditions teach that sex is somehow degrading, carnal, or base. They regard it as an evil necessary for the propagation of the human race, but it is not supposed to be pleasurable, and holy people are not supposed to indulge in it. This view is simply false. Sexual desire within marriage is proper. The purpose of the sexual relationship is for the consummation and strengthening of the union of a man and a woman, as well as for procreation. (See Proverbs 5:15-23; I Corinthians 7:1-5.) Those who forbid marriage are teaching false doctrine (I Timothy 4:1-3). Hebrews 13:4 summarizes the truth about the sexual relationship: "Marriage is honourable in all, and the bed undefiled: but whoremongers and adulterers God will judge."

Because most people in our society, including youth, have been exposed to explicit discussions of sexuality, we must be plain in presenting a biblical viewpoint. Within marriage, the ultimate form of sexual satisfaction as planned by God is sexual intercourse. Various aspects of foreplay and mutual stimulation are also acceptable if both marriage partners agree and find mutual enjoyment. (See Song of Solomon 7:1-13; 8:3.) A couple should not do anything that either considers to be unnatural, unclean, or degrading. (As a possible example, see Leviticus 20:18; Ezekiel 18:6; 22:10.)

Sex and marriage are sacred because they involve the lifelong union of two people and because they involve procreation. By the union of male and female, a child is born. This child is a joint creation with God, a soul that will live forever. God intends for a child to be born only within the protected environment of marriage.

Biblical Definitions of Sexual Sins

Under the law of Moses, various sexual transgressions were punished by death, demonstrating the seriousness with which God views such sins. Although every sin is dangerous and will result in eternal judgment, there is still something particularly serious about sexual sins. The reason is that they violate the sacredness of marriage. Those who commit fornication are joined together as one flesh—a physical, emotional, and spiritual union God intends to occur only in the context of a lifelong marriage relationship (I Corinthians 6:15-16). Other sins are committed outside the body, but fornication is a sin against one's own body (verse 18).

Unlike some other sins, once a sexual sin is committed there is no way to make full restitution or put the sinners back into their original status. Thieves may be able to return what they have stolen. Liars may be able to correct their lies. A sexual sin cannot be undone, and it can affect a person for life. Ministers can become disqualified from their position, because they must be blameless, the husband of one wife, and of good report

(I Timothy 3:2, 7; Titus 1:6). (See also Luke 9:62.) God will readily forgive those who repent of sexual sins, but these sins often cause serious and even irreversible consequences in this life.

The first general conference of the New Testament church accepted the Old Testament definition and prohibition of sexual sin. It seemed good to the Holy Spirit and to the church to identify the teaching against all forms of sexual immorality as one of the four necessary parts of the Jewish law that all Christians, including Gentiles, must continue to obey (Acts 15:19-29; 21:25).

The following Scriptures give us a basis for analyzing specific sexual sins: "Put to death your members which are on the earth: fornication, uncleanness, passion, evil desire, and covetousness, which is idolatry. Because of these things the wrath of God is coming upon the sons of disobedience" (Colossians 3:5-6, NKJV). "For this is the will of God, your sanctification: that you should abstain from sexual immorality; that each of you should know how to possess his own vessel [body—NIV] in sanctification and honor, not in passion of lust, like the Gentiles who do not know God; that no one should take advantage of and defraud his brother in this matter, because the Lord is the avenger of all such, as we also forewarned you and testified. For God did not call us to uncleanness, but in holiness. Therefore he who rejects this does not reject man, but God, who has also given us His Holy Spirit" (I Thessalonians 4:3-8, NKJV).

Let us identify various sexual sins that the Bible condemns.

Fornication, from the Greek *porneia*, means unlawful sexual intercourse or "sexual immorality" (NKJV). Due to the open sinfulness of our day, we must explain plainly that fornication means all sexual intercourse outside a biblical marriage, including oral and anal sex. The Bible recommends marriage as a way to avoid the temptation of fornication (I Corinthians 7:2). Many times the New Testament teaches against fornication. (See I Corinthians 6:13-18; Galatians 5:19; Ephesians 5:3; Colossians 3:5; I Thessalonians 4:3.) In English, when the word *fornication* is used in a restricted sense, it refers to sex involving unmarried people. The law gave the death penalty for this sin (Deuteronomy 22:20-21).

Adultery is prohibited by many passages of Scripture. (See Exodus 20:14; Leviticus 18:20; Deuteronomy 5:18.) Death was the penalty under the law for both parties in a case of adultery with a married woman (Leviticus 20:10; Deuteronomy 22:22). The word refers to sex where at least one party is married, but not to the other. Adultery appears in the lists of the sins of the flesh (Matthew 15:19-20; I Corinthians 6:9-11; Galatians 5:19-21).

Incest is sex between closely related people, such as between parent and child or between siblings. There were twenty laws defining this sin (Leviticus 18:6-18; Deuteronomy 22:30). A man who committed adultery with his father's wife was punished by death (Leviticus 20:11). This sin was present in the Corinthian church and needed to be judged (I Corinthians 5).

Child molestation clearly violates the foregoing teachings against fornication and adultery, and it often involves incest. Abuse of children will result in harsh judgment from God. (See Matthew 18:1-4; Luke 17:2.)

Bestiality, sex with animals, was punished by death for both the person and the animal involved (Exodus 22:19; Leviticus 18:23; 20:15-16; Deuteronomy 27:21).

Rape was punished by death (Deuteronomy 22:23-27).

Lust. Jesus taught, "Whosoever looketh on a woman to lust after her hath committed adultery with her already in his heart" (Matthew 5:28). Temptation that comes to the mind or eye is not sin in itself, but it becomes sin if we entertain it and allow it to develop into lust (James 1:14-15; Matthew 4:1-11). Based on the words of Jesus, if we look at someone who is not our spouse and begin fantasizing about or desiring sex with that person, we have committed sin.

Lewdness and uncleanness. In the biblical teaching against unlawful sexual lust and acts, the KJV uses several additional words: *concupiscence* (strong desire, especially sexual desire), *lasciviousness* ("lewdness" in NKJV), and *uncleanness* (impurity). (See Mark 7:22; II Corinthians 12:21; Galatians 5:19; Colossians 3:5; I Thessalonians 4:3-7.) The latter two words include lustful thoughts, speech, and actions. *Lewdness* refers to anything that promotes or gratifies sexual lust, whether or not a sexual act is committed. *Uncleanness* covers all sexual sin, and it includes perversion (Romans 1:24).

Lascivious or lewd activities include mutual sexual stimulation outside marriage, pornography, voyeurism, exhibitionism, and indecent exposure. Worldly places with a lustful atmosphere and worldly activities that arouse lust fall under this category. Books, music, movies, television, dancing, stories, and jokes can all be lewd.

Intimate embracing can be sexually arousing. Such activity between unmarried persons leads to lust and often to fornication. Thus, holding hands, hugging, and kissing are not appropriate for casual dating but should be reserved for serious relationships and should be carefully controlled. Any further intimacy must be reserved for marriage. It is wrong for unmarried couples to engage in intimate caressing or other sexual stimulation. Even between engaged couples, kissing and embracing should be controlled.

Pornography

Pornography is a serious problem in our day, especially since it is readily available on the Internet, mobile devices, cable television, videos, and DVDs, as well as in print. It is strongly addictive. To avoid this sin, it is important to place controls on these media and to maintain spiritual disciplines such as prayer, fasting, and Bible study. In addition, to overcome this sin, it is also important to become accountable to one's spouse and possibly to a mentor or prayer partner. The pastor can help to implement an appropriate system of accountability, control, and spiritual discipline.

Masturbation (Self-Stimulation)

The Bible does not say anything about masturbation, so we will look to general scriptural teachings on sexual matters. We can identify two potential problems: lustful fantasies and addictive behavior. Ultimately, this is a question that each individual will have to answer personally.

Jesus taught that if a man looks at a woman lustfully he has committed adultery with her in his heart (Matthew 5:28). Paul advised Timothy to flee youthful lusts, to keep a good conscience, and to keep a pure heart (I Timothy 1:19; II Timothy 2:22). Lustful, lascivious thoughts are contrary to the Word of God. At the least, fantasizing about sexual relationships with a particular individual other than one's spouse is contrary to the teachings of the Bible. Questions to ask are: Does masturbation lead one to entertain improper lusts and fantasies? Does masturbation make one feel guilty or defiled?

Another point to consider is the purpose of sex. God designed it to be an important component of the intimate personal relationship between husband and wife. Sex is meant to be a shared expression of joy and love. Thus, it seems that habitual masturbation or psychological dependence on masturbation is not God's plan.

Effeminate Behavior

Effeminate behavior is a sin that will keep men from inheriting the kingdom of God (I Corinthians 6:9-10). The KJV word is from the Greek *malakos*, which means "soft, i.e. fine (clothing), figuratively a catamite." A catamite is a boy kept for purposes of sexual perversion. In other contexts, this word is translated as "soft," for soft raiment or clothing (Matthew 11:8; Luke 7:25). The same passage also lists "abusers of themselves with mankind" (Greek, *arsenokoitēs*). The NKJV translates these two words as "homosexuals" and "sodomites," which are synonymous in English. The *Interlinear Greek-English New Testament* translates the first as "voluptuous persons" and the second as "sodomites."

The primary reference is to homosexual activity, but the use of two words instead of merely one is significant. Some scholars suggest that the intent is to encompass both the passive partner and the active partner in homosexual relationships. We conclude that these words prohibit all homosexual behavior as well as men looking, acting, or dressing like women.

In this regard, we note that Deuteronomy 22:5 prohibits both males and females from wearing clothing that pertains to the opposite sex, which in its most blatant form is called *transvestism*. (See chapter 8.) Similarly, men are to have short hair, while women are to have long hair (I Corinthians 11:14-15). (See chapter 9.) Clearly, God intends for there to be a clear distinction between the sexes. Men should not be effeminate and women should not be mannish in mannerisms, behavior, or dress.

Homosexual Behavior

Homosexual behavior, or sexual relations between people of the same sex, will prevent someone from inheriting the kingdom of God (I Corinthians 6:9-10). When it involves women, this sin is also called *lesbianism*. The law gave the death penalty for homosexual acts (Leviticus 20:13). These acts are an abomination—something that will keep people from Heaven (Leviticus 18:22; Revelation 21:27). Both prostitution and sodomy were so abhorrent that the money obtained by such activities could not be brought to the house of God (Deuteronomy 23:17-18). The price charged by a male prostitute was called the "hire of a dog" and was forbidden as an offering.

Homosexuality is called *sodomy* from the story of Sodom in Genesis 19:4-11. When two angels in the form of men visited Lot's house, the men of Sodom attempted to assault them sexually. They asked Lot to bring his guests out "that we may know them"—a biblical euphemism for sexual intercourse. (See Genesis 4:1.) When Lot refused, they threatened to do worse to him than to his visitors. They refused to take Lot's two virgin daughters instead of the angels. Finally, the angels pulled Lot into the house, shut the door, and struck the men with blindness. Even then, the men "wearied themselves to find the door."

Homosexuality is one of the major sins for which God destroyed the city. Some people claim that the men's sin was only their inhospitality rather than their homosexuality. Jude 7 refutes this notion, saying the people of Sodom sinned by giving themselves to sexual immorality and "going after strange flesh." (See also II Peter 2:6-22.)

A similar story occurs in Judges 19:22-25. Certain men of Gibeah in Benjamin, whom the Bible calls "sons of Belial," tried to assault a male guest in the town. They were appeased only when he allowed them to have his concubine, whom they raped until she died. The other tribes demanded that these men be executed, but the Benjamites protected them. A civil war resulted that almost completely destroyed the tribe of Benjamin.

Another Old Testament story shows that it is important to guard against the possibility of homosexual misconduct. Noah got drunk on wine one day and lay naked in his tent in a drunken sleep (Genesis 9:20-27). One of his sons, Ham, observed Noah's nakedness and told his brothers. The brothers, Shem and Japheth, went in backwards and covered their father. When Noah awoke, he "knew what his younger son had done unto him." He pronounced a curse on Ham, saying that Ham's offspring would be a servant of Shem and Japheth. The wording and the magnitude of the punishment indicate that Ham's transgression was serious—possibly involving homosexual lust or action.

Kings Asa, Jehoshaphat, and Josiah removed sodomites from the land of Judah in accordance with God's will and as a part of their reform programs (I Kings 15:12; 22:46; II Kings 23:7). One of Judah's great sins was allowing boys to be sold as prostitutes (Joel 3:3). Pagan religions of that day incorporated homosexuality and female prostitution in ritual worship. Some have argued that this was the only reason why the Old Testament condemns homosexuality, but this argument cannot account for the judgment upon Sodom or the strong teachings of the New Testament.

The New Testament church endorsed the Old Testament teaching against homosexuality when it announced that Christians must abstain from fornication, that is, all sexual transgressions as defined by the law of Moses (Acts 15:19-29).

Romans 1 includes homosexual conduct in its account of the step-by-step decline of the human race into sin. It states that all humans have an opportunity to know the existence and power of God. Therefore, they are without excuse if they refuse to acknowledge and worship Him (verse 20). Since they did not glorify Him as God, nor were they thankful, they began to worship images of His creation instead of Him (verses 21-23). As a result, God gave them up to uncleanness "to dishonour their own bodies between themselves" (verse 24). Since they worshiped the creature more than the Creator, God gave them up to "vile affections." The women changed the natural use of their bodies into something that is against nature, namely, lesbianism (verse 26). Likewise, the men left the natural use of the woman and burned in lust towards each other, "men with men working that which is unseemly" (verse 27). They did not like to retain the knowledge of God, so God gave them over to a reprobate (debased, depraved) mind (verse 28).

Homosexuality is contrary to nature, because it involves use of the body contrary to God's design. It thwarts God's purpose for instituting sexuality, namely, to operate in the context of marriage between a man and a woman. In that setting, sex is a strong bond that unites male and female in a complementary relationship, and it provides the means for procreation. Homosexuality does not advance either purpose.

Some apologists claim that homosexuality is natural because researchers have occasionally observed this behavior among animals. At most, this evidence would show that such behavior is bestial or animalistic, not a model for humans. We do not think that other common animal behaviors such as forced sexual intercourse, violent aggression, unprovoked killing, and cannibalism are appropriate for humans.

Romans 1 reveals that homosexuality is the final depravity that results when humans persistently refuse to worship God. It is the final outcome of worshiping the creation—that is, the body—instead of God.

This passage does not say that an individual who practices homosexuality is necessarily a greater sinner than others, however. Rather, it indicates that as human society moves further and further away from godly principles, there will be a greater incidence of homosexuality. It becomes more prevalent as society gets further from God, as homes and marriages break up, as men abdicate their responsibilities, as women usurp the male role, and as evil spirits are able to operate more freely. Homosexuality is not necessarily a sign of extraordinary individual sin, but it is a product and a sign of the evil age in which we live.

No one who practices homosexuality can inherit the kingdom of God (I Corinthians 6:9-10). As previously discussed, this passage uses two Greek words to define homosexuality—*malakos* and *arsenokoitēs*—which the NKJV translates as "homosexuals" and "sodomites." The word *arsenokoitēs* comes from the word *arsēn*, meaning "male, man," and *koitē*, literally meaning "bed" and by extension "sexual intercourse." This language is as clear and unambiguous as possible.

We find another condemnation of homosexuality in I Timothy 1:10 using the same Greek word, which is translated as "them that defile themselves with mankind" (KJV) or "sodomites" (NKJV).

In the Tribulation, Jerusalem will be called the city of Sodom and Egypt (Revelation 11:8). In other words, it will be the headquarters of sexual perversion and spiritual adultery.

The word *uncleanness* includes all types of immorality, perversion, and homosexuality as in Romans 1:24. The New Testament repeatedly condemns uncleanness. (See II Corinthians 12:21; Galatians 5:19; Ephesians 4:19; 5:3; Colossians 3:5; I Thessalonians 4:7; II Peter 2:10.)

Our study reveals that homosexual behavior is sinful. It is not an illness or an alternative lifestyle, although typically it becomes an addiction or a spiritual bondage. To those who repent and seek deliverance, God will give power to resist temptation and live a new life.

Likewise, *transgender* or *transsexual* behavior is sinful. These terms refer to people who live contrary to their biological sex or undergo a sex-change operation. When such people repent, they should seek ways to fulfill God's original plan for their lives once again. If this proves to be impossible, they can live in celibacy. (Perhaps the principle of I Corinthians 7:20-24 would apply here. See NKJV.)

Factors That Influence Homosexual Behavior

Certain factors can increase a person's susceptibility to homosexual temptations. Some characteristics of culture, personality, physique, background, or life experience can make a person vulnerable, just as some people are prone to alcoholism, promiscuity, or criminal conduct. But by God's grace, these factors can be overcome.

Science has not demonstrated that homosexuality is genetic in origin. It is not correct to say, "I was born a homosexual," or "God made me a homosexual." Homosexuality cannot be strictly hereditary, for throughout history those who were exclusively homosexual could not procreate and therefore could not pass on their genes to future generations. A few homosexual researchers have claimed to find features of brain structure or chemistry that they link to homosexuality, but if these characteristics indeed exist, they are most likely a result of homosexual activity rather than a cause. In the final analysis, if there were some biological component to homosexuality, it would simply demonstrate that human nature has been corrupted by sin, just as the Bible teaches.

In reality, conscious human behavior involves a complex interplay of biological, environmental, and psychological factors. Humans are not creatures of instinct, but they have the power to choose and regulate their conduct. While we cannot escape the power of sin except by God's grace, we can choose to act or refrain from acting in specific ways. If this were not so, there would be no point in outlawing various forms of criminal behavior.

It is true that some people become aware of homosexual thoughts and tendencies at an early age and do not remember a time when they consciously chose homosexuality over heterosexuality. Their thoughts and feelings were molded by factors early in life. It is helpful to identify such factors in order to help prevent and overcome homosexuality, but they do not provide any justification for continuing in this lifestyle.

Psychologists have identified a number of factors that help to shape homosexual behavior. Children are more likely to become homosexual if they are not able to identify with their same-sex parent but become excessively attached to the opposite-sex parent. For example, if a father is physically absent from the home, is grossly abusive, is ineffectual and weak, or is feared and hated, there is a greater chance that his son will identify with his mother. The same thing can happen when the mother is extremely affectionate but controlling or domineering.

In such situations, the boy may identify with the feminine role and may crave male approval and love. He may resent his mother's domination or feel inadequate in comparison to her, and then transfer these feelings to women in general. He may see all women as untouchable saintly figures like his mother. Or he may become so overly loyal to his mother that he cannot have a normal relationship with another woman. Any one of these reactions can lead to homosexuality.

Another key influence is early sexual experience. A childhood or youthful encounter with a homosexual can shape behavior later on, especially if the experience is perceived as normal or pleasurable. Children who are molested by same-sex persons may grow to think of such encounters as normal or to define their identity by such encounters. When youth undergo puberty and begin to develop sexual awareness, they can be strongly influenced by homosexual experimentation or seduction.

An early love affair that ends disastrously, including one that results in an illegitimate child or an abortion, may cause feelings of rejection, guilt, and fear that can push the individual away from the other sex. Feelings of physical inadequacy, sometimes stemming from physical or emotional problems, can do the same. Moreover, adolescent alienation is a powerful force. The lack of suitable same-sex friends and a lack of participation in typical activities of the same sex can create a need for companionship and acceptance that is later met by homosexuality. Alienation and ridicule from peers may also drive the adolescent into contact and relationships with homosexuals, who can easily influence him.

Women who have had abusive relationships with men sometimes retreat into lesbianism. They may feel safer with another woman or may feel that it is easier to understand and be understood by another woman.

When the prevailing culture condones and glamorizes homosexual behavior, it encourages experimentation and involvement. People who are struggling with their identity, people who are rebounding from a bad situation, and people who are jaded by their life of promiscuity can become candidates for the homosexual life. As Romans 1 teaches, when society rejects God, it descends into worship of the creation, which leads to worship of the body, which leads to sexual immorality and promiscuity. Sexual immorality leads to the breakdown of marriage and family. As marriages and families become dysfunctional and disintegrate, the factors that promote homosexuality become more prevalent.

At the same time, people find that sexual immorality does not provide the satisfaction and fulfillment that they expected. Thus, they place even more emphasis on sexuality, become more promiscuous, and seek new forms of immorality, all in a vain attempt to find satisfaction. This quest leads to an increase of all kinds of deviant sexual behavior, including multiple marriages, fetishism, sadism, masochism, hardcore pornography, child molestation, transvestism, bestiality, and homosexuality. Thus, the widespread practice and acceptance of homosexuality indicates that society has reached the final stage of degeneration from God's plan, just as Romans 1 explains. We have arrived at this point in twenty-first-century Western culture.

An understanding of these influences and processes can help leaders to prevent, correct, or at least counteract unhealthy situations. This understanding also helps people who are struggling with homosexual desires by showing them some of the contributing factors. Once they realize that they were not born a certain way but have been influenced by unhealthy relationships and negative events, they have hope for change. They can take responsibility for their actions and can begin to remold their lives. They can learn how to modify their thinking, habits, and behavior and, most of all, how to trust God for victory.

An understanding of these matters can also help parents to raise their children properly. For instance, we see how important it is for fathers to develop warm personal relationships with their children; for wives not to usurp their husbands' authority in the home; for children to have suitable same-sex companionship with their peers; and for parents, especially mothers, not to pamper, overindulge, or overprotect their sons.

We also realize that we cannot trust society or public schools to offer appropriate guidance in sexual matters. Instead, parents and churches must provide the necessary training in biblical truth, including the different roles of the sexes and the proper relationship between the sexes. We must teach our children and youth how to avoid unhealthy situations and how to deal with problems. We must protect them from unwholesome influences and experiences that can influence them in the wrong direction at a crucial stage in their lives.

Overcoming Homosexual Behavior

As we have already stated, psychological and environmental factors do not justify the practice of homosexuality. Every habitual sin can be influenced or encouraged by an unhealthy background and negative experiences. Adults still have the ability and responsibility to determine what is right and wrong and to choose what is right. Many people have overcome under similar circumstances, even those who were subjected to the same family and environment factors. Ultimately, through the Holy Spirit we receive power to be victorious in every situation as we learn to yield to God.

At the same time, we must recognize that homosexuality is a powerful force. First, it typically results from early life experiences that are hard to erase. Second, it has usually developed over a long period of time and has become an ingrained habit. Third, spiritual forces are involved, so people who want deliverance from homosexual desires need God's help.

While a person can make a decision to stop committing homosexual acts, in most cases deliverance from homosexual desires is a long, difficult process. As with all habitual sins, some people seem to experience a more complete eradication of unwholesome desires than others, but those who are delivered should be careful not to expose themselves to unnecessary temptation. Overcoming is accomplished by consistent prayer, walking in the Spirit, disciplining the mind, and obtaining godly support and counsel. The goal should be complete deliverance, which can be obtained through patience, a determination to overcome, and a total love for God. Psalm 37:4 is literally applicable: "Delight thyself also in the LORD; and he shall give thee the desires of thine heart."

The first step is to cease homosexual activities. The Bible defines homosexuality in terms of practice, so when people stop participating in homosexual acts and stop entertaining homosexual lusts, then they are no longer homosexuals. The next step is to seek deliverance from homosexual desires. The third step is for God to give the normal heterosexual desires that He intends for all to have. Those who have fallen into homosexual sin must not accept homosexuality as a basic part of their personality but must realize that it is a learned (whether consciously or unconsciously) habit that can be eradicated.

We should treat homosexuals like anyone else who needs God—namely, with respect and friendship. We should not look on them with ridicule or contempt, but we should show them Christian love and concern. We do not approve of their conduct, but we accept them as persons. We do not offer condemnation but encouragement and hope. (See John 3:16-17.)

Homosexuals may be sincere, hungry for God, and of good moral character in many ways. Often they are extremely lonely and desperate. They usually go through an agonizing period of self-hatred, depression, and despondency until their conscience becomes seared. Our challenge is to reach out to them in love and introduce them to the baptism of the Holy Spirit. Through this experience they will receive power to change. There is no need to exclude them from church services unless they try to entice others in the church to participate in their sin. This danger usually arises from people who claim to be Christians but hide their homosexual behavior and secretly try to involve others.

If young men struggle with effeminate tendencies, the pastor, youth pastor, or other approved leader should counsel, guide, and mentor them individually so that they can become more masculine in speech, mannerisms, and dress. In some cases, they simply have lacked appropriate male role models and training. They do not need to be used in leadership unless they make progress in this area. Young women who struggle with masculine tendencies need similar assistance.

At the same time, we need to guard against the spirit of suspicion. A man who seems to have some feminine mannerisms may not be homosexual. Just because he is more sensitive than most men or more talented in certain areas does not mean he is homosexual. Even if someone struggles with homosexual temptations, he should be respected if he resists them and refuses to act on them.

In short, we cannot stereotype people, nor should we assume, insinuate, or charge that someone is guilty of homosexual activity based simply on certain mannerisms. Some very masculine men are homosexual, so appearances can be deceiving. Of course, we should protect our children and youth from unhealthy influences and encounters. Pastors have the responsibility to guard the flock and to warn against sin.

We can overcome all forms of sexual temptation and sin, including homosexual behavior. Inside everyone is a latent desire for the opposite sex if only the layers of habit and experience can be removed. The Holy Spirit will give the power to overcome. Pastor and friends must patiently offer their support, and the person must pray continually. Most importantly, the person must have a sincere determination to change his or her life and a sincere desire to live for God.

Conclusion

Adultery, fornication, lust, lewdness, pornography, and homosexuality are great dangers today, for the prevailing spirits of the world always attack the church. Pastors must teach and preach against these sins. It is advisable to organize men's and women's meetings to address these issues. It is also good to hold meetings for youth to discuss dating, intimate embracing and caressing, fornication, homosexuality, and marriage. Some meetings need to be held separately for males and females with appropriate respective teachers such as the pastor and pastor's wife. We must meet the challenge of the end time in these areas!

Resources to assist in overcoming sexual lust, pornography, sexual addiction, and homosexual behavior are available from Focus on the Family, *www.pureintimacy.org*, and *www.beaconministries.net* (an Apostolic Web site dealing with homosexuality).

There are many cases of overcomers. Paul told the Corinthians, after listing fornicators, adulterers, homosexuals, and other types of sinners, "And such were some of you: but ye are washed, but ye are sanctified, but ye are justified in the name of the Lord Jesus, and by the Spirit of our God" (I Corinthians 6:9-11). We can conquer all sin, including sexual sin, through faith in Jesus Christ, heartfelt repentance, baptism in Jesus' name, the baptism of the Holy Spirit, and daily spiritual disciplines as we rely on the power of the Spirit.

Session 6

Discussion Questions

1. How does something as simple as the food we eat reflect a commitment to holiness?

2. Describe how the principle of separation from the world factors in when we consider the Christian's stance on alcoholic beverages.

3. Our culture has very open policies about acceptable sexual practices, yet God's Word specifically limits this to the role of husband and wife. Why do you think God so designed it?

4. Given God's clear view of homosexuality and yet our biblical directive to be kind as Christians, what is the proper response when we are confronted by homosexuality in the media, in the workplace, and with family members?

5. *The values and practical applications of holiness we have studied go against much of what our contemporary society promotes. How do we embrace separation and communicate our beliefs with a loving spirit?*

6. *As a result of all the sessions combined, put your personal statement of commitment to holiness in a single sentence.*

Afterword

The word *pursuit* indicates an ongoing attempt to attain something, and so it is in our effort to be holy. In every area of our lives, as we have studied throughout these diverse sessions, we must strive every day to let God's holiness work in us and to abstain from sin—a commitment that affects how we think, speak, dress, treat our body, and treat others.

This effort must be bolstered with prayer as we ask the Lord to show us places inwardly and outwardly where we need to make adjustments to present ourselves more effectively as "a living sacrifice, holy, acceptable unto God" (Romans 12:1). Also, we must spend time in the Word of God so it can guide us in how to make the needed changes in our lives and in how to make holy choices in our ever-changing world.

The word *pursuit* might also suggest something illusive about our effort to be holy. We understand after study, however, that we have clear Bible guidelines for living a life of holiness as we continue day in and day out to make decisions based on the principles of God's Word. Should we fail, as is possible with our imperfect human nature, we have the confidence that our holy God is also a God of love, faithful to forgive (I John 1:9). Such hope should propel us all the more in our pursuit to live a life of holiness as worship unto Him—separation from sin unto our loving, holy God.

Additional Study

The following sources from which this book was taken offer further information.

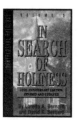

In Search of Holiness
By David K. Bernard and Loretta Bernard
This classic volume presents a synthesis of the fundamental principles of holiness as taught in the Scriptures.

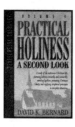

Practical Holiness
By David K. Bernard
With thorough research and historical perspectives, this volume investigates the theology of holiness and presents practical applications for topics such as dress, hair, abortion, divorce, and stewardship of the body.

On Being Pentecostal
By David K. Bernard and Robin Johnston
For some people "Pentecostal" is a new word. This book surveys the core doctrines of Oneness Pentecostalism and presents what it means to be Pentecostal.

Visit: *www.pentecostalpublishing.com*

Works by David K. Bernard:

Pentecostal Theology Series
Vol. 1: The Oneness of God*
Vol. 2: The New Birth*
Vol. 3: In Search of Holiness (with Loretta Bernard)*
Vol. 4: Practical Holiness
A Study Guide for The Oneness of God
A Study Guide for The New Birth
A Study Guide for In Search of Holiness
A Study Guide for Practical Holiness
(Each volume can be purchased in hardback with Study Guide included)

Biblical Theology (Other)
A Handbook of Basic Doctrines*
Doctrines of the Bible (ed. with J. L. Hall)
In the Name of Jesus
Justification and the Holy Spirit
On Being Pentecostal (with Robin Johnston)
The Oneness View of Jesus Christ
Spiritual Gifts*
God's Infallible Word
Understanding God's Word

Practical Theology
The Apostolic Life
Growing a Church
The Pentecostal Minister (ed. with J. L. Hall)

Commentaries
The Message of Colossians and Philemon
The Message of Romans

Booklets
Essential Doctrines of the Bible*
Essentials of Oneness Theology
Essentials of the New Birth*
Essentials of Holiness
Understanding the Articles of Faith
Bible Doctrines and Study Guide

Church History
A History of Christian Doctrine, Vol. 1: The Post-Apostolic Age to the Middle Ages
A History of Christian Doctrine, Vol. 2: The Reformation to the Holiness Movement
A History of Christian Doctrine, Vol. 3: The Twentieth Century
Oneness and Trinity, AD 100-300
The Trinitarian Controversy in the Fourth Century

CD-ROM
Pentecostal Digital Library, Vol. 1: Complete Works by David K. Bernard
Preaching the Apostolic Faith
Teaching the Apostolic Faith
Pentecostal Pulpit Series, Vol. 3: David K. Bernard (with audiovisual CD)
An Introduction to Apostolic Pentecostal Theology (4 books)

*In Spanish (en Español)

www.pentecostalpublishing.com